W9-BXV-709

PHOTOS **Jurjen Drenth** TEXT **Martijn de Rooi**

Schiermonnikoog
Terschelling
Ameland
Vlieland
Spijk
Delfzijl
Groningen
Groningen
Leeuwarden
WADDEN SEA
Texel
Friesland
Sneek
Hindeloopen
Heerenveen
Sloten
Assen
Bourtange
Den Helder
Drenthe
Emmen
North Holland
IJSSEL-MEER
Giethoorn
Alkmaar
Hoorn
Kampen
NORTH SEA
Edam
Volendam
Lelystad
Zwolle
Zaandam
Marken
Flevoland
Overijssel
Haarlem
Amsterdam
Almelo
Lisse
Deventer
Hilversum
Apeldoorn
Enschede
Leiden
Utrecht
Amersfoort
Scheveningen
The Hague
Utrecht
Zeist
Ede
Gelderland
Hoek van Holland
Delft
South Holland
Gouda
Arnhem
Doetinchem
Rotterdam
Kinderdijk
Nijmegen
Dordrecht
's-Hertogenbosch
GERMANY
Zierikzee
OOSTERSCHELDE
Breda
Westkapelle
Veere
Roosendaal
Tilburg
North Brabant
Middelburg
Zeeland
Bergen op Zoom
Helmond
WESTERSCHELDE
Eindhoven
Venlo
Weert
Limburg
Roermond
BELGIUM
Sittard
Maastricht
Heerlen

**New Visions of the Netherlands**
A Dutch Publishers publication

**Text**
Martijn de Rooi

**Photography**
Jurjen Drenth

**Design**
Maarten van der Kroft

**Printing**
Scholma Druk, Bedum

**ISBN 978-90-76214-16-0**

First printing, August 2013



**Contact**
Dutch Publishers is a trade name of The Ad Agency, Alphen aan den Rijn, the Netherlands. Phone (0)172 449 333. E-mail: info@theadagency.nl. Visit us at **www.dutchpublishers.nl** and **www.dutchshop.nl**.

**Holland promotion**
Find further inspiration on our websites DutchImage.nl and Dutchshop.nl. All images from this book are available here, as well as other products, gifts and services, both for individual purposes and b-to-b.

**Captions page 4-9**
Page 4-5: Amsterdam's picturesque canals. Page 6-7: Tulips in bloom. Page 8-9: Winter in Kinderdijk, in the province of South Holland.

# New Visions of the Netherlands

In 1997, we published *Visions of the Netherlands*, a highly successful book presenting a broad impression of the Netherlands and its inhabitants. Now, sixteen years later, we present an updated version, *New Visions of the Netherlands*. Like *Visions*, it explores the many facets of the country as seen through the eyes of one of her best photographers, a craftsman whose favourite subject is the land he lives in.

The 250 photos in *New Visions* give a modern and realistic image of the country. They show the Netherlands as it is now, and how people see it every day. The book does not confine itself to the capital, Amsterdam, which is so popular with visitors, but also shows dozens of less visited places, some of which, had they been situated elsewhere, might well have become world famous. Furthermore, it shows the Dutch in their everyday environment – at work, at play and in their favourite pub.

The Netherlands is a hospitable country, easy to travel around and visited yearly by about 11 million tourists and business people. We hope that this book will inspire many – both Dutchmen and visitors – to learn more about the country and, in learning, develop their very own visions of the Netherlands.

1

# Water

## No country in the world is more strongly associated with water than the Netherlands. It's often said that 'the Dutch stand in it and it pours down on their heads' – a comment as pointed as it is humorous.

One might think that they aren't an enviable place to live in, these wetlands, but nobody understands the art of taming water better than the Dutch. They barricaded their coasts with dams and dykes and created a refuge where life was no longer dictated by the rhythm of the tides.

**The Low Countries**

Much of the Netherlands is a delta formed by three big rivers – the Rhine, the Maas and the Schelde – and from ancient times, ingenious solutions have had to be found to help the people keep their heads above water. Over a quarter of the country, inhabited by some 60% of the population, lies below sea level and without adequate safeguards it would disappear beneath the waves. Without the protection of dunes and dykes, two thirds of the country would flood should water levels rise. The lowest point of the Netherlands (6.76 metres below sea level) is in Nieuwerkerk aan den IJssel. In a country whose name translates appropriately as the 'Low Countries', this title is a source of pride.

The low-lying position of the Netherlands intrigues and fascinates many foreigners. Land below sea level, what does that look like? Many imagine the Low Countries as marshy, half-submerged pastureland. However, a surprise awaits them at Schiphol, the national airport, because although it lies four metres below sea level, Schiphol is actually as dry as a bone. Only its name is a reminder of the days when there was a notorious bay here – a graveyard ('scheepshol') for sailing ships.

**Champions at controlling water**

Huge waterworks were necessary to make the Netherlands dry and habitable, and the Dutch were forced to become specialists in hydraulic engineering. Nowadays, they are regarded internationally as the champions in water control and lead the field wherever there is something to salvage, dredge or build in foreign waters. When it comes to impoldering, land reclamation, constructing bridges and harbours, the Dutch can compete with the best. This sterling reputation is partly due to Hans Brinker, the young literary hero of American origin, who made history by sticking his finger in a hole in the dyke, preventing catastrophic flooding.

The struggle against the water has been going on for centuries, but in modern times, one event in particular greatly influenced its course. In 1953,

The coast of Ameland, one of the five inhabited Friesian Islands (Wadden Islands). The islands form a barrier between the North Sea and the Wadden Sea and have traditionally had to endure the power of wind and water. As a result of prevailing winds and ocean currents, the islands are 'migrating' eastwards. On the west side, they are disappearing little by little under the water while on the east side, large sandbanks arise.

the south-west provinces of the country were ravaged by a freak flood tide driven by gale force winds and 1,835 people lost their lives. Again the traditional enemy had demonstrated just how vulnerable the Netherlands is, and to prevent a repetition, the Dutch were once more forced to call upon their engineering genius.

They struck back with the Delta Works, a massive complex of water control mechanisms designed to guarantee safety for the South Holland and Zeeland islands and which, at the same time, reduced the length of the North Sea coast from 1,080 to about 360 kilometres. The jewel in the crown of the Delta Works is the storm surge barrier in the Nieuwe Waterweg, known as the 'eighth wonder of the world' – a later addition that was completed in 1997 and which is a hydraulic engineering masterpiece of the first order.

**Terps and polders**

The struggle against the watery enemy was originally fought with modest means. Between 500 BC and 650 AD the then Friesian population of the North and West-Netherlands erected several thousand artificial refuges, up to 15 metres in height, called 'terps' (mounds), on which they built houses and villages. The sea level continued to rise and heightening these mounds was a recurring ritual. To some extent, this occurred naturally as rubbish and manure accumulated.

Under pressure from the rising waters, the settling of the soil, peat extraction, the increasing population and countless catastrophes both large and small, the Dutch mastered the art of controlling the waters. From 1000 AD onward, dykes were constructed and this created the opportunity to drain stretches of land, but the technology to carry out large-scale projects was still absent.

It was eventually developed in the 15th century and took the form of the windmill, something which today is still a characteristic feature of the Dutch landscape. The perfected windmills, connected in series, were able to pump large lakes dry. The hydraulic engineer and windmill builder with the rather apt name of Leeghwater ('Empty water')

1

2

The Wadden Sea is a unique nature reserve and an important recreational area popular with mud-flat walkers at low tide **{3}**.

The Loosdrechtse Plassen **{1}** are an important nature reserve and recreational area too. The seven 'plassen' (lakes) in the province of North Holland were created between the 14th and 19th centuries when layers of peat were 'cut' from peat bogs. When dried, this was used as fuel. The lakes are a popular attraction for water sports and skating enthusiasts.

The canals of Amsterdam **{2}** are a world-famous attraction. The city's 17th-century 'Grachtengordel' (Canal Belt) features numerous historical bridges and buildings, and is a UNESCO World Heritage Site. Many Dutch cities boast historic canals, traditionally serving as both waterways and lines of defence.

Along the Dutch coast, lighthouses such as the striking Paard van Marken (Horse of Marken) from 1839 **{4}**, show ships the way.

1

God created the world, but the Dutch created the Netherlands.

was very much in vogue in the 17th century as, with the aid of dozens of windmills, he transformed one lake after another into a polder.

The most spectacular reclamations, however, date from after the introduction of the steam-driven, and later the electric-powered, pumping station. These are the Haarlemmermeer and IJsselmeer polders, possibly the largest polders in the world. The IJsselmeer project was the work of the hydraulic engineer Cornelis Lely, the brain behind enclosing the Zuider Zee. Soon after the province of North Holland had been ravaged by heavy flooding, he was given the green light for the construction of the 30-kilometre long Afsluitdijk, which was completed in 1932. The Zuider Zee – a huge bay cut by the sea – became an inland lake – the IJsselmeer – which was then partially reclaimed. Lely's services were so highly regarded that Lelystad, a city in one of the new polders, was named after him.

How much the modern inhabitants of the Netherlands owe to men like Leeghwater and Lely is demonstrated by the fact that about 20% of the country's land area has been reclaimed from the waters. Their achievements are summed up briefly but eloquently in the saying 'God created the world, but the Dutch created the Netherlands.'

**An eternal struggle**

The threat of flooding is less obvious than it used to be. Behind the proud Delta Works, designed to prevent catastrophes which statistically occur once in ten thousand years, a sense of safety reigns. Still, the Dutch recognise that the 'Thousand Years War', as the struggle against water is sometimes called in the province of Zeeland, is eternal.

The 17,500 kilometres of dykes and

The most striking symbol of the eternal battle with the sea is the former island Schokland {1}, which has been located in the Noordoostpolder since 1942. Before that time, it had to wage a bitter battle for existence. Time and again, parts of the land had to be yielded to the Zuider Zee (Southern Sea) and the 650 inhabitants fell into dire poverty.

In 1859, the island was evacuated by order of the government. However, thanks to the enclosure of the Zuider Zee in 1932 and the partial impoldering of this body of water, Schokland managed to survive. Instead of lying above sea level, it now protrudes from the flat polders. This 'Island on Dry Land' is a UNESCO World Heritage Site.

In many other places, things did not turn out as well. In the province of Zeeland alone, there are 117 'drowned' villages that were literally wiped off the map over the centuries. On the banks of the Oosterschelde, a single church spire {2} is all that remains of the village of Koudekerke, which disappeared into the waves in the 17th century.

Eighteenth century gravestones of seamen in Hollum, on the island of Ameland, are proof of the price that had to be paid to take part in the greatest Dutch commercial adventures {3}. In those days, the people from Ameland were involved in whaling, a cold adventure that many people paid for with their lives.

other weirs, and the thousands of polders both large and small – altogether, 60% of the territory – demand continuous maintenance and management. The latest technology is put to large-scale use in this process and there is also intensive experimentation with new, often spectacular methods, such as the construction of a large sand bar off the coast of The Hague in 2011, known as the 'zandmotor' (the sand engine). Over a period of 20 years, the wind, the waves, and the currents will cause the sand to wash over a section of the coast to create a natural reinforcement of the beach and dunes.

In the last 20 years or so, overflowing rivers and dyke movements led to new insights and measures, too. Riverbeds were deepened, dykes were moved or even cut across and agricultural areas were 'given back to nature' in order to create 'water overflow zones' – a form of 'depoldering' which caused protests among farmers and others. At the same time, land reclamation continues. For example, in 2012, construction was completed on Maasvlakte 2, a 2,000 hectare extension of the port of Rotterdam.

**Useful and pleasant**

But water is not only the Netherlands' enemy. It also has its useful and pleasant aspects – for example, you can sail on it – and the Dutch have always exploited this very well. Throughout the centuries, they played a leading role in shipping, shipbuilding and overseas trade. Waterways have always been widely used for transport and for a long time, there was no method of transport in the world more reliable than the Dutch canal barge. In times of need, the Dutch even made the water their ally as they barricaded themselves behind the Hollandse Waterlinie, a wide stretch of flooded land bordered by a series of fortifications. Water also played an important role in the protection of cities and fortresses.

In a country which is almost one fifth water, it is no wonder that water also fulfils an important recreational role, in winter, too, when the Dutch surrender en masse to what is almost a sacred national custom – skating. It is hard to find a place which does not have a view of a lake, pool, river, canal, waterway, ditch, stream or small harbour. There is good reason why a swimming diploma is the first in a long series of certificates that every resident of the Netherlands is expected to obtain during the course of his or her lifetime.

## Terps

The 12th century church of St Nicholas in Hijum stands like a sentinel over the surrounding landscape. The village of Hijum, in the province of Friesland, is an example of a 'terp' village. 'Terp' is an ancient Friesian word, originally meaning 'village', but in modern times used to designate artificial dwelling mounds. These structures were raised from 500 BC onwards, especially by the Friesians, in the north of the country, along the North Sea and former Zuider Zee coasts and in the Rhine and Maas river plains.

The first terp builders had settled on small natural hillocks in the region where the land met the sea. As the sea level rose, the 'islands' had to be heightened from time to time. To some extent, this occurred naturally through the accumulation of rubbish and manure, but there was plenty of clay about which was also used for this purpose. Terps were sometimes as much as 15 metres in height. Originally they would contain a single house; but gradually villages and even towns were built on them. Leeuwarden, the capital of Friesland, for example, was created from three terp villages.

It is estimated that several thousand of these 'refuges' existed in Friesland, Groningen and North Holland. Many have been damaged or have completely disappeared. This has several causes, one of which was the excavation of the fertile soil. The terp at Hijum was partly excavated around 1900 with only the area around the church remaining untouched.

## The struggle against the water

An eternal struggle against the water is the price the people of the Netherlands pay for their 'low' country. In order to keep their heads above water, the Dutch were forced to become specialists in hydraulic engineering. The terp (see pages 16-17) was the first milestone in this process; and dyke construction, which took place after about 1000 AD, was the second. Villages like Uitdam **{1}** exist by the grace of their protective dykes.

More modern works are examples of impressive engineering ingenuity. The Afsluitdijk **{3}**, a 30-kilometre long link between the provinces of North Holland and Friesland, featuring a statue of its creator Cornelis Lely, was completed in 1932. The Delta Works, a huge complex of dams and bridges protecting the delta region of the south-west, are world famous. The Zeelandbrug **{6}** measures 5,022 metres. Upon its completion in 1965, it was the longest bridge in Europe. The Delta Works project was crowned in 1986 by the completion of the unique, nine-kilometre long storm surge barrier in the Oosterschelde **{4}**. The former artificial 'work' island Neeltje Jans, situated halfway to the barrier, is now a popular tourist attraction.

The 255-kilometre long belt of dunes along the North Sea coast is also impressive in its own way **{2}**. Along with the adjacent wide, sandy beaches, it forms a natural barrier against the water. Every year, around 12 million cubic metres of sand are sprayed onto the beaches to reinforce the coastal landscape.

Even the inland part of the country bears witness to the eternal struggle against the water. A monumental example of this is the sluice from 1828 which connected the port of Edam with the then Zuider Zee **{5}**.

1

2
3
4
5
6

1
HENGELO 1913
2

3

4

5

## Polders

Large parts of the Netherlands have been reclaimed from the waters through the process of impoldering. Originally, as in the case of the polders on the former island of Noord-Beveland in the province of Zeeland **{4}** and parts of Krimpenerwaard in the province of South Holland **{5}**, this was done with the aid of windmills. Nowadays, the windmill's work has been taken over by modern pumps. Oostelijk Flevoland **{1}** is one polder created with the aid of such pumps.

Haarlemmermeer in North Holland was the first polder to be drained using steam-driven pumping stations; colossal machines which enabled the Dutch to perfect the art of impoldering. The Cruquius **{3}**, which began operating in 1849, was one of them. The huge lake was drained in 1852, and today the polder, which is the location of the national airport Schiphol, is situated four metres below sea level.

The Cruquius, located south of the city of Haarlem, is now a museum. It contains the largest steam machine in the world. Other steam-driven pumping stations, like De Hooge Boezem in Haastrecht **{2}**, which dates from 1872, were also turned into museums. Here, as is the case in some other places, the monumental machines rely on volunteers to keep them running smoothly.

## Rivers

The Maas **{5}** is one of the so-called ‘great rivers’ that cut across the Netherlands from east to west. The Maas, Rhine and Waal form a natural border between the traditionally predominantly Catholic south and the largely Protestant north of the country. The waterways have traditionally been of great importance for trade and transport. The same is true of the IJssel, a tributary of the Rhine which flows from the south to the north, and was already an important trade route in the Middle Ages.

Despite the rise of road transport, the major rivers continue to be of great economic importance and Dutch inland waterway vessels are a familiar sight deep in the heart of Europe **{4}**. The fleet of 7,000 Dutch inland waterway vessels is the largest and most modern on the continent.

The rivers and other waterways, with their total length of 6,200 kilometres, dominate the landscape. The backdrop of rivers infuses many areas with a timeless romantic quality, as is emphasised by images of the Vecht **{2}** and of pollard willows lining the flooded water meadows of the Waal river **{1}**. In many places, such as in the Overijsselse Vecht **{3}**, hand-powered rope ferries are used to cross rivers.

1

2

3

4

5

## Sailing vessels

In a land of wind and water, sailing vessels are a familiar sight. Among the most impressive are the 500 or more ships of the 'Bruine Vloot' (Brown Fleet), which until the 1950s were still employed in the fishing industry, the coastal trade and on inland waterways. The name refers to a traditional custom in inland navigation – tarring the nets and sails, so they would last longer.

When the fleet was modernized, these sailing vessels – ranging from 'modest' tjalks to seagoing clippers and schooners – were pensioned off, but from the 1960s onward they were restored to their former glory by private individuals. Now they are hired out to parties of passengers who want the experience of an 'old-fashioned' sail on the IJsselmeer **{2}**, the Wadden Sea, the North Sea or the Friesian lakes. In ports such as that of Hoorn, mighty sailing ships are a familiar sight **{1}**.

High points in the lives of the skippers are the sailing races. The best known sailing event is the 'skûtsjesilen', the regattas in Friesland for 'skûtsjes' built in that province. These cargo boats were traditionally used to transport peat, manure and other goods within the province. Nowadays, they compete against each other in regattas, including during the annual 'Sneekweek' **{3}**, a very popular event on the Friesian lakes next to Sneek, which is the largest of its kind in Europe.

1

2

3

## Living by the water

Many Dutch people have a view of the water from their living room. This is certainly true of the inhabitants of historical cities such as Amsterdam **{3}**, which is crisscrossed with canals, and the small city of Sloten in Friesland **{2}**, which is completely bisected by one. A number of municipalities are experimenting with new ways to live by the water. One example of this is the Eilandenbuurt neighbourhood **{1}**, which was built at the turn of the 21st century in Almere, a town in the province of Flevoland renowned for its modern architecture.

For years, thousands of Dutch people have literally lived on the water in houseboats. The number of houseboats by far exceeds the 10,000 official moorings, but 'illegal' houseboats are often tolerated. In Amsterdam alone, there are already more than 2,500 houseboats **{3}**.

1

2

3

## The water as an ally

The Dutch have traditionally used the water to defend their towns and country. By the Middle Ages already, castles and other buildings were surrounded by canals. A fine example of a moated castle is the 14th-century Ammersoyen Castle in Ammerzoden, in the province of Gelderland **{3}**.

Villages and cities were also surrounded by canals for defence. Some – such as the beautiful townships of Naarden, Hulst, Heusden, and Bourtange – became known as fortresses by virtue of their impressive ramparts and (partial) star-shaped arrangement. The 16th-century defensive work Bourtange **{1}**, in the province of Groningen, was originally occupied only by soldiers, but it soon attracted craftsman, farmers and traders and grew into a fortified town which reached its zenith half way through the 18th century. It fell into disrepair, but in the second half of the 20th century, it was beautifully restored to its 18th-century condition.

The sea fort Pampus, in the IJmeer **{2}**, dates from more modern times. Constructed in 1895, it forms part of what is known as the Defence Line of Amsterdam (Stelling van Amsterdam), which is a 136-kilometre long defensive ring around the city made up of 42 forts and four batteries. If the capital was threatened with attack, the land outside the line could be flooded. The Defence Line, which is a UNESCO World Heritage Site, has never been put into practice. Fort Pampus is open to the public.

## Recreation

For many Dutch people, water is an important source of leisure and entertainment. As soon as the weather permits, they flock en masse to the beaches **{3, 7}** for walks, sunbathing, or a cool dip, or they search out other bodies of water for swimming **{8}**, sailing **{5}**, canoeing **{4}**, kite surfing **{9}** or for going on a pleasant boat trip **{6}**. A typical rural tradition is 'slootjespringen', where the trick is to try to get to the other side of the ditch, dry, by way of a pole vault **{1}**. In winter, Dutch people flock en masse to the water to ice skate and traditionally, children learn to skate with the help of a chair **{2}**.

1

2

4

5

7

8

3

6

9

'Boat farmer' in the characteristic 'water village' of Giethoorn, in the province of Overijssel. Giethoorn and the surrounding villages were originally settlements for peat cutters. This explains why the 'road network' consists of a series of canals – the dried peat was transported along them. Boats are still the principal form of transport in the picturesque 'Venice of the North'; and cars are conspicuous by their absence.

The watery landscape around Giethoorn – including the Weerribben-Wieden National Park – owes its present form to the peat cutters. The expanses of lakes and other bodies of water are mostly shallow, which is why farmers and countless tourists use flat-bottomed boats, called 'punters', steered with a wooden pole. Taking these boats out is called 'punting'.

2

# Landscape

## Many overseas visitors are astounded at the exceptional versatility of the Dutch landscape.

They expect a small, flat and densely populated country like the Netherlands, of which virtually every centimetre has been manipulated by man, to be monotonous. However, nothing could be further from the truth. Countries that boast such a wide variety of landscapes within such a small area are rare, and remarkable as it may seem, this diversity is largely the result of human intervention.

**Exceptional versatility**

The term 'Dutch landscape' immediately conjures up images of vast polders and grassy meadows under high cloudy skies, as depicted in the paintings of so many Dutch masters. Perhaps we might also picture a landscape of lakes dotted with white sails or the sand dunes and broad beaches of the North Sea coast. But we would certainly not imagine the coniferous forests of the Veluwe, the heathlands of Drenthe or the hills and half-timbered cottages of Limburg. Yet these landscapes are just as 'Dutch' as the polders, the meadows, the lakes and the sand dunes.

The most important characteristic of the Dutch landscape is not the monotony people associate with a flat, green, watery land, it is its unusual level of diversity. This versatility is further enhanced by the changing of the seasons, which continually alters the aspect of the landscape.

The enthusiast, then, will find much to enjoy in the Netherlands. Nature itself has made its contribution, of course, but the country's exceptional diversity is largely due to the work of the Dutch who, over the centuries, have reshaped the contours of the land they live in.

**The influence of nature**

Geologically speaking, the Dutch landscape is relatively young. It was largely created during the Ice Age and the Holocene period which followed it, and in which we still live. The simplest way to imagine the Netherlands is as a depression in the earth's crust which was gradually filled with sediment from the large rivers and the sea, debris transported by the land ice, and sand and loess carried by the wind.

All this resulted in a varied natural landscape. Besides extensive sandy regions in the east and south of the country, there are large areas of river and sea clays and peat and, in the far south-east, loess and chalky soils.

Although in comparison with most other countries the Netherlands can justifiably be called 'as flat as a pancake', there is a striking difference in elevation between the east ('high Netherlands') and the west ('low Netherlands'). The east is more than five metres above sea level and large areas of it are even as much as twenty metres above sea level. There are also higher areas along the west coast, specifically the sand dunes formed by the North Sea and the wind. These extend out across the eight Wadden Islands to the north of the Dutch mainland. These islands, popular with beach enthusiasts, lovers of peace and quiet and those interested in plant and

A typical Dutch polder landscape: a windmill in the Eilandspolder conservation area in the province of North Holland. The polder consists of pastureland with an abundance of water and bird life. Originally, it was an island, hemmed in between large lakes that would later be reclaimed – hence the name. Windmill De Havik (The Hawk) was constructed in 1576 to drain excess water from the polder – a function that was taken over by a pumping-station in 1918, since which time The Hawk has been in retirement.

bird life, were once part of a long chain of dunes until the sea broke through and created the Wadden Sea, which now separates the islands from the mainland.

Another characteristic feature of the landscape is the ridges, such as the Utrechtse Heuvelrug, the Veluwe and the Sallandse Heuvelrug, which were forced up by the ice during the Ice Age before the previous one. The southern part of the province of Limburg, i.e. the far south-east of the country, is also hilly. This is a transitional region between the Belgian Ardennes and the Low Countries. Here, on the border with Belgium and Germany, lies the Vaalserberg, which, at a dizzying 322 metres, is the highest point of the Netherlands.

**Cultivated landscape**

But the influence of nature fades into insignificance when compared to the works of man, who shaped and recreated the natural landscape into one of order and cultivation. Originally, the Dutch adapted themselves to the landscape, but as the population grew and technological development progressed, they turned their attention to the 'wastelands'.

They cut down the extensive forests of the sandy soils and drained the inaccessible marshes of the clay and peat regions. They dug out the peat, creating lakes, which were again partly drained. The result was a continually changing mosaic of man-made landscapes in which a rich variety of flora and fauna developed. Furthermore, man's intervention, both on land and sea, drastically changed the contours of the Netherlands. A comparison between old and modern maps makes this obvious at a glance.

In the past century, this development has taken place at an increasing pace and with a negative effect – a reduction in biodiversity – as a result. An enormous growth in population – at the beginning of the 20th century the Netherlands had about 5 million inhabitants, and in 2013 some 16.8 million – went hand in hand with increasing prosperity and mobility, the scaling-up of agriculture, industrial expansion, a growing infrastructure and an increasing need for recreation. This resulted

A typical Dutch dune landscape on the Wadden island of Schiermonnikoog **{2}**. Dunes are one of the few features of the Netherlands not created by human intervention.

Fields with bales of hay in the province of Groningen **{1}**, the characteristic hills of South Limburg **{3}**, and a typical Drenthe heathland with a herd of sheep **{4}** illustrate the versatility of the Dutch landscape.

The friendly, rolling landscape of South Limburg is literally a high point of the Netherlands. The hills form a transitional region between the Belgian Ardennes and the flat Netherlands. The half-timbered houses are also characteristic of this region.

On the barren sandy soil of Drenthe province and elsewhere, extensive heathlands came into being through human intervention. Due to an increasing need for agricultural land, wool and fertiliser, farmers cut down sizeable areas of woodlands to create farmland and to graze large herds of sheep and other livestock. Due to intensive farming and grazing, the ground became more barren and the heathlands were created. With the arrival of artificial fertiliser and cheap foreign wool, both the heathlands and the sheep lost their function. In the 19th and 20th centuries, the heathlands were largely converted to agricultural land and coniferous forests. Nowadays, many of the remaining heathlands are protected and the remaining herds of sheep help maintain them through grazing.

in a fundamental change in the use of space and the relationship between city and countryside. The Dutch landscape became a neatly ordered entity, designed at the drawing board and completely adapted to the primary needs of the population.

### New nature

From circa 1970 onward, the Dutch increasingly became convinced that this far-reaching regulation of the landscape was taking place at the cost of the quality of life. It was not only the disappearance of 'original nature' that was regretted (at the most only a small percentage of the landscape can be described as such), but there was also concern at the disappearance of characteristic landscape forms and species of plants and animals. Increasing pollution was also a source of concern.

A growing number of social organisations campaigned for measures to turn the tide, with success. Thanks partly to their efforts, measures such as creating nature reserves, protecting landscapes and planting forests have been taken. Species of animals – from certain breeds of cattle to beavers – which had disappeared from the Netherlands have been reintroduced into their original habitats.

The Dutch government's current environmental policy is focused on the conservation of a network of nature reserves, including the twenty national parks, and the creation of 'new nature' by, for example, converting agricultural land into nature reserves and restoring specific landscapes to their former glory. Connection zones are created between nature reserves, so that plants and ani-

The charms of the landscape: pollard willows beside a frozen stream at Vlist in the province of South Holland **{1}**, a snow-covered tree in De Sallandse Heuvelrug National Park in Overijssel **{2}**, and a field behind a tree-studded dyke near Kwadendamme in Zeeland **{3}**.

Nature enthusiasts will find much to enjoy in the Netherlands.

mals are not confined. Measures such as these are characteristic of the strong manipulability-mentality that is characteristic of the Dutch when it comes to the design of their country – if there is not enough nature left, they will create it!

The management of nature reserves rests with various bodies and organisations – farmers and other private individuals also play a role – and varies from place to place. Sometimes nature is left to run its course, while in other cases active maintenance is performed. In many nature reserves, 'grazers' such as sheep, European bison, semi-feral horses (koniks), heck cattle, roe, fallow deer and red deer are utilised to contribute to management.

**Conflicting interests**

There is no doubt that the defenders of nature and the landscape have achieved important successes, certainly in alerting the Dutch to the unstable balance between quality of life and non-quality of life. It is partly due to them that, in every respect, the Netherlands is a country fit to live in, with an exceptional diversity of landscapes and a surprisingly large number of sparsely populated and beautiful spots.

Nonetheless, 'quality of life' will always remain a matter of balancing interests, and these are often conflicting ones. In such a densely populated country as the Netherlands, a country that also sets great store on prosperity and a high standard of living, tough choices are unavoidable.

This dilemma is graphically illustrated by the traditional furore over plans for the construction of new urban developments, roads and railway lines, especially in areas such as the so-called Green Heart of the Randstad. This region, until now more or less untouched, lies literally at the heart of the great agglomeration which includes the major city centres of Amsterdam, Rotterdam, The Hague and Utrecht.

Yet another example is the neverending debate concerning the growth of the national airport Schiphol. Because of this, thoughts turn from time to time to the construction of a second Schiphol, perhaps on an artificial island in the North Sea.

These examples clearly show that quality of life, almost by definition, is at odds with the desire or the necessity for economic growth. In a densely populated country like the Netherlands, you simply cannot have your cake and eat it – even though you may still have an unshakeable belief in your ability to create anything you want to create.

The Dutch landscape at its most recognizable: water, meadows and a beautiful cloudy sky near Schermerhorn in the province of North Holland.

## Flowers

The Netherlands is a land of flowers. People devote a great deal of attention to their gardens and no house will be called a home without a bouquet of flowers on the table. At the beginning of May, the orchards blossoming in the fruit-producing region of the Betuwe are a splendid sight **{1, 7}**. The bulb fields are the basis of a flourishing export trade, and are also a popular tourist attraction **{2, 4, 5}**.

It is no wonder that throughout the world the Netherlands is associated with flowers – particularly with the tulip, the symbol for everything that is Dutch. In a certain sense, however, the Netherlands is displaying another man's finery, as the tulip is not native to the country, but was imported from the Turkish Ottoman Empire in the 16th century. A wide variety of new species were cultivated in the Netherlands from these imports. The Dutch word for tulip – 'tulp' – is itself imported, being derived from the Turkish word 'tulbend' (turban).

The most important bulb-growing regions are the Kop (Head) of North Holland and the area between Haarlem and Leiden, which contains centres such as Noordwijkerhout and Lisse, where Keukenhof, the largest flower garden in the world and an important tourist attraction, is located **{3}**.

At the end of April, the bulb fields are reminiscent of a giant mosaic. After they have flowered, the heads are cut off mechanically **{6}**, a process that strengthens the bulbs and helps to ensure the Netherlands' blossoming reputation does not wither.

## Protected landscape

The Netherlands has many hundreds of protected nature conservation areas and twenty national parks. The parks comprise ecosystems characteristic of the exceptional versatility of the Dutch landscape: dunes, woodlands, heathlands, fenlands, tidal waters, stream valleys and pools. Each of the parks has its own inhabitants, from unusual breeds of birds, butterflies, reptiles and amphibians, to deer, badgers, beavers, otters and seals.

De Hoge Veluwe National Park in the province of Gelderland **{1, 4}** comprises diverse landscapes: heathlands, grassy plains, shifting sands and deciduous and coniferous forests, each with its own diversity of flora and fauna. The larger inhabitants of the park include fallow deer, roe, mouflons and wild boar.

The history of the area typifies the radical way in which the Dutch manipulate nature to suit them. Like large areas of the Netherlands, the sandy soil of the Veluwe was originally wooded. As a result of extensive wood felling for agriculture and ship building, heathlands and shifting sands were created. New woods were planted to counter the dust clouds, but when their growth threatened to overwhelm the shifting sands and their characteristic flora and fauna, steps were taken, which included cutting down a large section of forest at the beginning of this century. The park now forms an impressive mosaic of the types of nature the area has hosted.

The park is also a unique cultural attraction. The Kröller-Müller Museum houses a world-famous collection of visual arts, the highlight being a large number of works by Vincent van Gogh, and a large sculpture garden. The collection belonged to Mr and Mrs Kröller-Müller, the former owners of the area. They also commissioned the construction of the charming Sint-Hubertus hunting lodge, designed by the famous architect H.P. Berlage. In addition, the park boasts the Museonder, the world's first underground museum, which provides a glimpse into the world beneath the earth's surface.

Stunning woodlands along a winding stream are a feature of Landgoed Gossink in Winterswijk, in the province of Gelderland **{2}**. The Dwingelderveld National Park in Drenthe **{3}** includes the largest interconnected wet heathlands in Western Europe and consists of woodlands and shifting sands, as well as rolling heathlands with small lakes and pools.

1

2

3

4

# The four seasons

The wide diversity of the Dutch landscape is enriched even more by the changing of the seasons. Each season stamps its mark on the landscape. Still snowscapes, like this one near Haastrecht in the province of South Holland **{1}**, are typical of winter. For most inhabitants of the Netherlands, this is the season for skating and enjoying the cosiness of home, but many heave a sigh of relief – particularly after a long, hard winter – when the advent of spring colours the landscape; literally, such as in this tulip field in Burgervlotbrug, North Holland **{2}**. Summer reveals the Netherlands at its greenest and sunniest. This is the season for those who enjoy rustic scenes, as here near Zweeloo in the province of Drenthe **{3}**. Finally, autumn, the season of falling leaves, has a charm all of its own. The woods and heathlands of the Planken Wambuis nature reserve in Gelderland **{4}**, with their wonderful colours, look like something out of a fairytale.

3
4

The romance of the woods: the estate of Heidestein in Zeist in the province of Utrecht, which forms part of an extremely diverse nature reserve. In the distant past, there were extensive forests throughout the Netherlands. Over the course of time, these forests made way for agricultural land and heathlands. For a long time, the Netherlands even had fewer woodlands than almost any other country in Europe. However, thanks to nature conservation and replanting, the situation has been greatly improved.

The provinces of North and South Holland probably derive their names from the woodland vegetation of the past – it is likely that over time, the name 'Holland' evolved from the phrase 'holt land' (woodland). In the 17th century, the province of Holland (at that time it still had not been divided into North and South Holland) played a dominant role in the then Republic of the Seven United Provinces. This is the reason why today the Netherlands is still frequently referred to as 'Holland', even though North and South Holland are just two of twelve Dutch provinces.

## The Wadden Sea

The Wadden Sea, hemmed in between the north coast and the Wadden Islands, is a unique nature reserve and the habitat of over 10,000 mostly rare plant and animal species, as well as the annual stop over point for millions of migratory birds. Its diverse landscapes – from mud flats and sandbanks to mussel beds and dunes – and the changes that occur within them according to the rhythm of the tides, make the Wadden a genuine biological treasure trove. It is with good reason that the Wadden Sea is on the UNESCO World Heritage List.

The Wadden Sea takes its name (literally: 'sea that can be waded through') from the fact that it drains out at low tide. Then, sporty nature lovers hike across its largely dried out mud flats with the assistance of guides. Many mud-flat walkers cross over from the mainland to one of the Wadden Islands.

Another unique activity connected to the tidal flows is the so-called 'drying out'. Skippers manoeuvre their flat-bottomed vessels over sandbanks; when the tide goes out, the boats come to rest on dry mud flats and passengers have the opportunity to explore the area **{1}**.

To the north, the Wadden Sea is bordered by a belt of eight Wadden Islands, of which five are populated: Texel, Vlieland, Terschelling, Ameland **{3}** and Schiermonnikoog. The islands are what remain of a long row of dunes that the North Sea broke through. Over time, this caused the peat bogs behind the dunes to become part of the sea – the Wadden Sea.

Due to their peaceful surroundings, beautiful beaches, dunes and nature reserves, the islands are popular with both nature lovers and holidaymakers. The photos depict the small village of De Kocksdorp on the northern point of Texel **{2}** and the village of West Terschelling with its prominent lighthouse, the Brandaris **{4}**.

## Animals

A selection of typical countryside inhabitants proves that not only the landscape, but also animal life, has many facets. Cows **{2}** and horses **{6}** are permanent residents of the pasturelands. Swans are a familiar sight in the waters – elegant birds that are not averse to a long walk once in a while **{1}**. You are likely to encounter herds of sheep on the heathlands, such as here in the province of Drenthe **{4}**. By grazing on grasses, young trees and bushes, they help maintain the heathlands. A number of other animals are also used to maintain landscapes, including this Highland cow, seen at work here in the Zuid-Kennemerland National Park **{3}**. Seals are a much-loved sight in various waters, particularly the Wadden Sea **{5}**. The photo was taken in Ecomare, a nature museum, an aquarium and information centre on the Wadden island of Texel, as well as one of the centres where sick and weak seals are cared for temporarily.

1

2

3

4

5

6

3

# Architecture

For many foreign visitors, the charm of Dutch cities resides in their small size and their often strong cosmopolitan and historic character. However, even lovers of modern architecture get their fair share in the Netherlands.

Dutch towns and villages are just as efficiently arranged as the surrounding countryside, but what is particularly striking is the lack of any large metropolis. In the eyes of most foreigners, even the big cities are no more than provincial towns, though they do have a strong cosmopolitan and historic character. Many people feel that it is the authentic combination of 'smallness' and character that gives the Netherlands its charm.

**A miniature country**

Many foreigners are of the opinion that everything in the Netherlands is on a small scale, beginning with the country itself. According to international criteria, even the cities are tiny – for instance, the largest city in the Netherlands, Amsterdam, has only 802,000 inhabitants.

Dutch buildings are also relatively small, or in any event, low. Tall buildings are comparatively scarce – there are practically no skyscrapers whatsoever. Finally, many think that Dutch houses and gardens are extremely cramped, but it is all a matter of what you are used to. The Dutch themselves, even though they are among the tallest people in the world, think they are fine.

**The oldest structures**

The oldest structures in the Netherlands are in the province of Drenthe. They are 52 communal megalithic tombs, called 'hunebedden', erected between 3400 and 3100 BC by a farming community. They consist of enormous granite boulders and vary in length from 4.5 to more than 22 metres, with the largest located near the hamlet of Borger. Two more 'hunebedden' are to be found in the province of Groningen.

Later inhabitants left less impressive traces. At the beginning of the Christian era, the Romans established settlements in dozens of places along the rivers Rhine and Maas. They called the crossing places in these rivers 'traiectum', and it was from this word that names of cities such as Utrecht and Maastricht were derived. Maastricht is one of the three oldest cities in the Netherlands. The other two are Nijmegen and Voorburg.

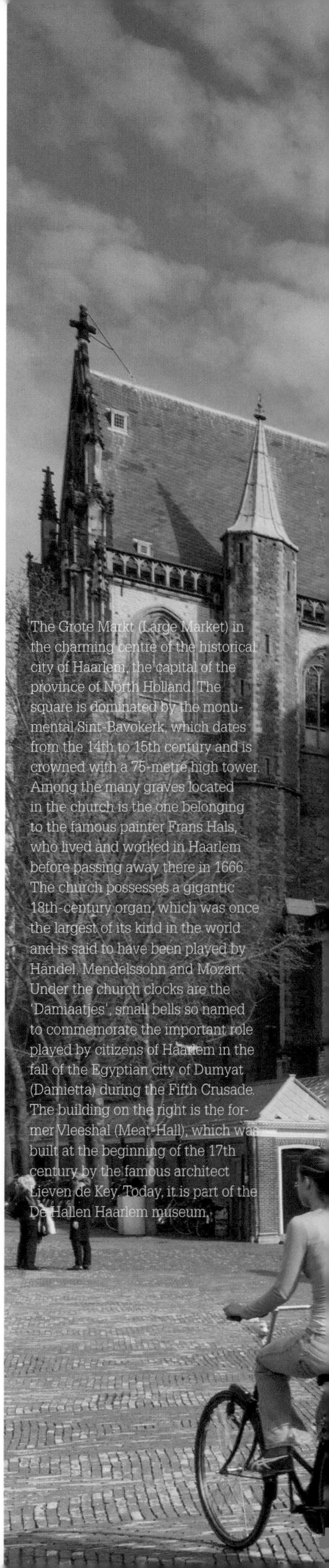

The Grote Markt (Large Market) in the charming centre of the historical city of Haarlem, the capital of the province of North Holland. The square is dominated by the monumental Sint-Bavokerk, which dates from the 14th to 15th century and is crowned with a 75-metre high tower. Among the many graves located in the church is the one belonging to the famous painter Frans Hals, who lived and worked in Haarlem before passing away there in 1666. The church possesses a gigantic 18th-century organ, which was once the largest of its kind in the world and is said to have been played by Händel, Mendelssohn and Mozart. Under the church clocks are the 'Damiaatjes', small bells so named to commemorate the important role played by citizens of Haarlem in the fall of the Egyptian city of Dumyat (Damietta) during the Fifth Crusade. The building on the right is the former Vleeshal (Meat-Hall), which was built at the beginning of the 17th century by the famous architect Lieven de Key. Today, it is part of the De Hallen Haarlem museum.

GIFTSHOP
SOUVENIRS
DE
HAL
LEN

A 'hunebed' (megalithic tomb) in Havelte in Drenthe **{2}**. The 'hunebedden' are the oldest monuments in the Netherlands. The graves, built of 'erratic blocks' (boulders transported from what is now Scandinavia during the second Ice Age), were originally covered with earth.

The 14th-century Zuidhavenpoort in Zierikzee **{3}**, one of the three gates of this Zeeland town which have stood the test of time. The cupola on the roof of the Zuidhavenpoort houses the oldest working carillon in the country. Zierikzee is one of the many Dutch cities in which the relics of a turbulent history can still be plainly seen. It was an important trading centre and seaport as early as the 13th century and it remained so until the 18th. Time then stood still until the first tourists knocked on the city gates in the 1970s. The part of the city inside the canals, dating from the Middle Ages, has retained most of its old charm.

A modern high rise in The Hague **{1}**, part of a mixed-use development of office buildings and housing called De Resident (The Resident). The 104-metre-high Castalia building features two peaked roofs, reminiscent of traditional Dutch architecture, and was designed by Michael Graves. The 88-metre-high Zurichtoren (Zurich Tower) to the left was designed by Cesar Pelli. The tallest building is the 142-metre-high Hoftoren (Court Tower), designed by Kohn Pedersen Fox Associates.

If you want to see the Netherlands in a couple of hours, then a visit to the miniature city of Madurodam in The Hague **{4}** is in order. Built on a scale of 1:25, Madurodam gives a fascinating image of 'the structured Netherlands'. Dozens of imposing buildings and city quarters, ranging from a 'hunebed' and windmills to examples of modern architecture, have been carefully 'rebuilt'. Madurodam was founded in 1952 with money donated by the parents of the Dutch-Antillean George Maduro, who died in a German concentration camp in 1945.

Many people feel that it is the authentic combination of 'smallness' and character that gives the Netherlands its charm.

4

**Historic cities**

Utrecht and Maastricht are two of several dozen Dutch cities that are considered to be small according to international standards, but which are nonetheless extremely charming and historically interesting. Not only the towns themselves, but also their museums – the Netherlands has the highest 'density' of museums in the world – offer the visitor a detailed picture of the past.

The development of several cities, including the capital city Amsterdam, can still be traced. A canal would be dug around the historic heart, building would take place outside it and this extension to the city would again be encircled by a canal. Some towns were also enclosed by ramparts, walls and bastions for defence. A limited number of bridges and gates gave access to these places, which sometimes took the form of a real fortress, characteristically in the form of a star. Splendid examples of this are Naarden, Hulst, Heusden and Bourtange.

Over the centuries, and particularly since the emergence of motorised traffic, characteristic historical elements have disappeared from many townscapes. In Utrecht – in the Middle Ages and for a long time the largest city in the Netherlands – and other cities, many of the canals were filled in to facilitate the construction of roads and shopping centres. Currently, several towns are restoring these canals to their former glory.

**Modern cities**

Rotterdam – founded in the 13th century and now the fifth largest seaport in the world – is a surprising omission from the list of historic cities. At the beginning of the Second World War, it was largely destroyed by German air raids and today it is a classic example of a 'modern' city. It is no coincidence that the Netherlands Architectural Institute is established here, in a rather remarkable building in which a variety of exhibitions are held. Rotterdam is home to a number of spectacular modern buildings.

Those who enjoy somewhat older architecture can still find several interesting buildings that survived the bombardment, especially in the municipality of Delfshaven, the former port of the city of Delft that was annexed to Rotterdam. Other famous examples are the 17th-century Schielandshuis, the town hall completed in 1920, and Hotel New York, situated in the former head office of the illustrious Holland-America Line that was built at the start of 20th century. The Van Nelle factory dates back to 1930 and is a wonderful example of the

Traditional architectural differences can still be clearly seen.

A striking element of the façades of historic houses in Amsterdam and other cities are the stone tablets, which made a general appearance in the 17th century {1}. However beautiful or original, these tablets were not only intended as decoration. At the time, there were no street signs and house numbers and they functioned as name boards and addresses, displaying the name or profession of the person living in the house, or the name of the house.

The charming village of Persingen, in the province of Gelderland, is one of the smallest villages in the country and has only 80 inhabitants. However, it was once a thriving settlement, to which the church, which dates from the 14th and 15th centuries, bears witness {2}.

The (considerably larger) Friesian village of Oldeboorn, which is situated on the banks of the river Boorne and famous for its crooked church spire, had become prosperous at an even earlier date thanks to trade {3}.

The monumental wooden buildings from the Rozenwerf neighbourhood on the former island of Marken date from the 18th and 19th centuries {3}. Storm floods ripped Marken away from the mainland in the 13th century, but the island was connected with it again by way of a dyke in 1957. As a result of prolonged isolation, many traditions of the previously insular fishing community can still be seen, which is why the island is now a major tourist attraction.

architectural style known as Het Nieuwe Bouwen ('New Building').

The new towns built on reclaimed land in the polders are also world renowned. The best examples are Almere and Lelystad, dating from the 1960s and planned down to the last paving stone. Experimental ideas in building and living were given free rein here, and Almere in particular has much to offer in the field of modern architecture.

**Other modern architecture**

The Netherlands has an abundance of splendid 20th-century architecture. Housing and office developments, bridges, stadiums and other constructions have attracted international admiration. Dutch Railways, which has produced dozens of much-talked-about designs for railway stations, must also be mentioned in this context.

In addition, there are a large number of striking buildings in styles that are never, or only rarely, seen outside the Netherlands. In particular, there is increasing appreciation for buildings from the period between 1910 and 1930, designed by H.P. Berlage and representatives of two prominent movements, the Amsterdam School and De Stijl (The Style).

Berlage, one of the Netherlands' most famous architects, achieved international recognition and was the inspiration behind – and pioneer of – modern Dutch architecture. His buildings are simple, functional and built in brick. Among his best-known designs are the Commodities Exchange on the Damrak in Amsterdam (1903), the Sint-Hubertus hunting lodge in De Hoge Veluwe National Park (1920) and the Gemeentemuseum (Municipal Museum) in The Hague (1935).

Architects of the Amsterdam School were also fond of using brick. In contrast to the simplicity of Berlage's work, this movement is noted for its highly imaginative designs. Brick was often only used in the towers, decorative doorways and fanciful curved features in the façade, behind which was a rigid design in concrete.

Spectacular buildings of the Amsterdam School can still be admired in many places and are increasingly being designated as listed monuments. Examples are Van der Mey's Scheepsvaarthuis (Shipping House) in Amsterdam (1916), De Klerk's public housing in Amsterdam's Spaarndammerbuurt (1918) and Kramer's Bijenkorf department store in The Hague (1926), as well as many bridges, country houses and villas in Bergen and Het Gooi, among other places.

A completely different perspective was held by a group of artists known as De Stijl, who propagated abstract design, based on straight lines and the use of only a few primary colours. The group included the painter Mondriaan, the painter-architect Van Doesburg, and architects such as J.J.P. Oud, Rietveld, Van 't Hoff and Wils. Their most famous buildings include the Rietveld-Schröder house in Utrecht (1924) and Oud's De Unie café in Rotterdam (1925).

**The countryside**

There is also much to enjoy architecturally in the Dutch countryside. There are more than 3,000 villages in the Netherlands and a remarkable variety of village types – a phenomenon linked to the great variation in landscape forms.

For example, there are coastal villages, terp villages built on mounds, villages built around central squares, and ribbon villages. Despite modernisation, in many places the original link between village and landscape can still be clearly seen.

This also applies to local architectural differences. In scores of villages, fixed colour combinations and particular materials were used, examples of which can be found along the IJsselmeer and in the Zaanstreek, among other places.

Farms and windmills, very 'Dutch' constructions which are found particularly in the countryside, come in all shapes and sizes. The most important types can be seen in the Open Air Museum in Arnhem, which gives an imposing picture of life in the countryside. This museum is a true paradise for visitors who want to taste the authentic charm and 'smallness' of the Netherlands.

2
3
4

The atmospheric Voldersgracht in Delft in the province of South Holland. It is believed that the famous artist Johannes Vermeer was born along this canal in 1632. Whether this is true or not, the fame of Delft – which in any event was a great source of inspiration for the painter who was far from famous when he was alive – is none the less for it.

A more doubtful milestone in the history of Delft was the murder of William of Orange, the leader in the struggle for an independent Netherlands, in 1584. The 'Father of the Fatherland' is buried in the Nieuwe Kerk (New Church). Nearby, in the Oude Kerk (Old Church), lie other prominent victims of these turbulent times: the naval heroes Piet Hein and Maarten Tromp. Hein was born in Delfshaven, Delft's seaport, later annexed to Rotterdam, and worked for the West India Company which, like the Dutch East India Company, had offices in the city.

Overseas trade was indirectly responsible for the city's fame. Chinese porcelain imported from East Asia was the source of inspiration for the china industry which went on to provide the whole of Europe with 'Delft Blue'. This china is still the trademark of Delft, although the original Asian motifs have long been replaced by the characteristic cityscapes which make Delft one of the most beautiful historical cities in the Netherlands.

Grandcafe De Sjees

## Windmills

Miller Sopke Vergouw casting off his self-built windmill De Windjager (The Wind Hunter) in Oostzaan, North Holland **{5}**. The windmill is undoubtedly the most characteristic Dutch building, although the machinery was invented in the Middle East. If the Netherlands is renowned as a country of windmills, it is because the Dutch were unbeatable in their knowledge of making the best use of them.

For centuries, the Dutch depended on the wind for their livelihoods. While Dutch merchants were busy sailing the seas, the windmills back home were helping to drain the polders and to create and maintain a versatile industry. On the threshold of the Age of Steam, the country had 11,000 windmills. Of these, a thousand or so remain. A small number are still in daily use, while over a hundred mills are kept in operation at set times by amateur millers.

The most impressive collection of polder mills can be found at Kinderdijk in South Holland **{4}**. This site is home to nineteen 18th-century windmills, which were used to prevent the drained Alblasserwaard from flooding. The Kinderdijk mills are a UNESCO World Heritage Site and a famous tourist attraction. Polder mills can be seen all over the country, such as in the Friesian village of Tjerkwerd, for example, where a windmill dating from 1882 looks exactly like a Delft Blue painted scene when combined with a snowy backdrop **{2}**.

The biggest concentration of industrial mills can be found along the Zaanse Schans in North Holland, another famous tourist attraction (see page 116). The windmill De Kat (The Cat) is the last of the 55 paint mills which once stood along the river Zaan, and the only working paint mill in the world **{3}**.

The tallest surviving windmills are located in Schiedam in South Holland. The windmill De Nieuwe Palmboom (The New Palm Tree), dating from 1781, is one of the 20 windmills that milled raw materials for the hundreds of distilleries that made the famous Jenever from Schiedam **{1}**. The windmill is still partly functional and also serves as a museum. Very close by, there are another four gigantic windmills, including De Noord (The North), the highest classical windmill in the world.

1

2

3

4

5

The Netherlands boasts a great number of impressive castles. Kasteel Schaloen **{1}** in Oud-Valkenburg, Limburg, was built around 1200, but has a thorough renovation at the end of the 19th century to thank for its current form. This renovation was led by the influential architect Pierre Cuypers, who also developed the Rijksmuseum and the Central Station in Amsterdam. The castle is entirely made of marl and is now a hotel. Kasteel De Haar in Haarzuilens, Utrecht, is the biggest castle in the Netherlands **{2}**. It was built in the 14th century, but gained its current form at the turn of the 20th century as a result of major renovations, again by Pierre Cuypers. The castle, with its breathtaking interior and spectacular art collection, all surrounded by French-style gardens and an English landscaped park, is open to the public.

The Netherlands has a large number of different types of farm. Many farms and their buildings are already full of character because of their location, such as this one in the ancient village of Zweeloo in Drenthe **{3}**. The monumental Haubargs in the Beemster, the former inland sea that was dried in the beginning of the 17th century by the famous hydraulic engineer Leeghwater and then divided up according to a strict geometric pattern, are distinctly unusual. Many of these farms, such as De Eenhoorn (The Unicorn), which dates from 1682, in the village of Middenbeemster **{4}**, were built by rich Amsterdam merchants, who used them as summer houses and bedecked them with façades similar to those of their canal houses. The Beemster is a World Heritage Site because of its unusual history and significance.

2
4
6

The Amsterdam merchants also invested their profits in building 'Buitenplaatsen' (summer residences), including those along the river Vecht. A large number of these have been conserved, including Vegtvliet in Breukelen, Utrecht **{6}**, which was built in 1670 according to a design by Philips Vingboons, who was the most famous architect in Amsterdam at the time. In a completely different style is the former estate of Heidepark in Doorn (Utrecht), which was christened Hydepark in 1885 by its new owners, restructured and given a facelift. The then estate was destroyed in the Second World War and today, the beautiful outbuildings and surrounding park **{5}** are owned by the Protestant Church and serve as a conference centre.

## The Big Four

There are four 'big' cities in the Netherlands – Amsterdam (802,000 inhabitants), Rotterdam (617,000), The Hague (508,000) and Utrecht (325,000). All four are part of what is known as the 'Randstad', a huge agglomeration in the west of the country, where the largest part of the population lives. Although they are not very far apart, each of these cities has its own distinctive character.

The capital city, Amsterdam, is an open air museum. The historical city centre is the largest of its kind in Europe. Its famous 17th century Canal Belt with its monumental canal houses and 8,000 protected monuments is a UNESCO World Heritage Site. A typical view is that of the Montelbaanstoren and the adjacent canal, both of which form part of the fortification works from 1516 **{1}**. The city has 1,281 bridges – probably more than any other city in the world – and the 17th-century Magere Brug (Skinny Bridge), spanning the Amstel, is the most famous **{2}**. The ambiance in the city is cosmopolitan, free and democratic. The typical Amsterdammer is open, humorous and self-confident, or, as their arch-rivals in Rotterdam would say, 'arrogant'.

Rotterdam, as befits a seaport, is known as a city of hard workers whose motto is 'not words, but deeds'. Rotterdam is also the most modern city in the Netherlands, a focal point of modern architecture which dares to experiment. Since the dramatic German bombardment of May 1940, which destroyed the entire city centre, Rotterdam has been feverishly building towards its future. At the Oude Haven (Old Harbour) in the city centre, the famous cubic apartments, designed by architect P. Blom, look out over terraces and the Willemsbrug **{3}**. The ambiance of old Rotterdam can still be found here and there, especially in Delfshaven, the former port of the city of Delft, which was annexed to Rotterdam in 1886 **{4}**.

The Hague, the 'lovely city behind the sand dunes', is the seat of government and the stateliest city in the country. The beautiful palaces and houses and great squares have an unmistakable air of distinction. Although impressive new building projects are taking up increasing space, the centre still has much of the ambiance of the days when the Counts of Holland established their courts there in the 13th century. The Binnenhof (Inner Court), from where the Counts wielded the sceptre over Holland, is particularly eye-catching and is the current seat of government and parliament **{page 66, 1}**. The little tower in the centre houses the Prime Minister's office. The building on the left is the 17th-century Mauritshuis, now a world-famous museum housing a unique collection of paintings. The Hague is also known as the 'Legal Capital of the World' and the 'City of Peace and Justice', a reputation that comes from the large number of international organisations and institutions that are situated here. The Vredespaleis (Peace Palace), which was built in 1913, houses the Permanent Court of Arbitration and the International Court of Justice **{page 66, 2}**.

Utrecht is the least well-known of the four. It was originally a Roman town. In the Middle Ages, it was the seat of a powerful bishopric and a prosperous trading centre, and for long afterwards it was an important fortified town. The atmospheric canals and ramparts in the centre date from this period. Oudegracht **{page 67, 1}** is in the heart of the city and its banks were lined with buildings as early as 1200. Between 1300 and 1500, the wharves, characteristic of the Utrecht canals, were built. These were linked to the canal houses by deep cellars. These restored wharves and cellars, with their restaurants, bars and pavement cafés, play an important role in the leisure life of the city. Seen in the background is Utrecht's most eye-catching feature, the 14th-century, 112-metre-tall Domtoren, the tallest church tower in the country. Some of the most atmospheric streets in the city are behind the Dom Tower **{page 67, 2}**.

E PLAN-C

Dommelsch Bier

## Architecture 1900-1940

The world-famous Rietveld-Schröder house in Utrecht **{1}**, completed in 1924, was built according to the radical design by G. Rietveld. It is a classic example of the architecture of De Stijl (The Style). The building is a UNESCO World Heritage Site.

The Town Hall of Hilversum in North Holland **{2}**, completed in 1931, is W.M. Dudok's best-known work and shows the influence of two important architectural movements: the Amsterdam School and Het Nieuwe Bouwen ('New Building').

The Bijenkorf department store in The Hague, completed in 1926, was designed by P. Kramer in the style of the Amsterdam School **{3}**.

The Grote Zaal (Main Exchange) of the former Commodities Exchange in Amsterdam features a statue of Mercurius, the Roman god of commerce **{4}**. The monumental building (1903) is probably H.P. Berlage's best-known work. It reflects, just like Berlage's design for De Burcht (see pages 70-71), his interest in the architecture of the medieval town-halls of Italian city states. The rich and – for a bastion of capitalism – rather unusual decoration was the result of his cooperation with the poet Albert Verwey, who, like Berlage, was a socially-minded artist.

Between approximately 1915 and 1920, a number of interesting houses in the style of the Amsterdam School were erected in the Spaarndammerbuurt in Amsterdam. In 1921, the architect Michel de Klerk completed Het Schip (The Ship), which was one of his 'palaces for the working classes' in the area **{5}**. Never before was so much effort put into the architecture of homes for the working class. Since 2001, Museum Het Schip has been housed in this building, which is dedicated to public housing and the Amsterdam School.

EEN GROEP BONDSLEDEN
JARIG BESTAAN VAN DEN
VOOR

The central hall of De Burcht (The Castle) in Amsterdam was built between 1899 and 1900 by order of the General Diamond Workers' Union of the Netherlands, and was designed by the famous architect H.P. Berlage, who also designed the interiors.

The first trade union building in the Netherlands had to become a monument for the workers' movement and it was essential that the building radiate power, harmony and beauty. Following the example of the Italian council houses from the time of the city-states, which Berlage had studied, it was given a solid and sober brick facade. Because of its robust design, it quickly became known as the 'castle of the workers' and entered history as De Burcht.

Through a sombre portal, visitors enter a surprisingly light-filled hall, an effect that symbolises the future that the workers' movement desired (i.e. going from the darkness into the light). Yellow glazed bricks add to the effect. The murals in the building are by Richard Ronald Holst, who was a dedicated socialist, as was Berlage.

## Modern architecture

The Stedelijk Museum in Amsterdam **{1}**, famous for its amazing collection of modern art, is situated in a neo-Renaissance-style building dating from 1895 and designed by Adriaan Weissman. It has undergone extensive renovations and, at the same time, it received a new wing that was opened in 2012. This wing was designed by Benthem Crouwel Architects and is commonly known as De Badkuip (The Bathtub).

The 90-metre-high office tower in Amsterdam which bears the appropriate name The Rock (2009) **{2}** was designed by Erick van Egeraat according to a style the architect describes as 'modern baroque'.

The post-modern ING House in Amsterdam **{3}** was completed in 2002. It was designed by Meyer & Van Schooten and is the head office of ING Verzekeringen. It was nicknamed De Klapschaats (The Klapskate), De Kruimeldief (The Dustbuster) and Het Strijkijzer (The Iron).

The façade of the Inntel Hotel in Zaandam **{page 74, 1}**, designed by Molenaar & Van Winden/WAM architects, is a highly imaginative compilation of traditional Zaandam wooden houses. The designers called the building, which was completed in 2010, an example of 'fusion architecture', which connects the present and the past, and modernity and tradition.

The science centre NEMO in Amsterdam seems to rise out of the water of the Oosterdok like the bow of a ship **{page 74, 2}**. The building, opened in 1997, was designed by Renzo Piano. It is built above the IJ tunnel, its exterior is clad with copper and a large 'town square' has been constructed on the roof.

The Red Apple in Rotterdam **{page 74, 3}**, with its striking, 120-metre-high residential tower, was designed by KCAP Architects. The building contains both residences and offices, and was completed in 2009.

The Wave, a residential complex in Almere (Flevoland) dating from 2004, was designed by René van Zuuk **{page 74, 4}**. It takes its name from its aluminium-plated wave-shaped façade.

The Rijksmuseum in Amsterdam **{page 74, 5}**, with its fantastic collection of Dutch paintings from the Golden Age, belongs to the crème de la crème of museums. The impressive building was designed by Pierre Cuypers and finished in 1885. It underwent a full renovation between 2004 and 2013 according to the design of Antonio Cruz and Antonio Ortiz. The photograph shows a giant chandelier that the duo designed for the atrium.

The Gas Union's office in Groningen, designed by Albers and Van Huut, is a fine example of organic architecture **{page 75}**.

1

2

3

4

The Erasmus bridge in Rotterdam, designed by Ben van Berkel and also known as 'The Swan', is a creation as elegant as it is daring. It fits perfectly into this bastion of modern and innovative architecture. Completed in 1996, the bridge is 808 metres long and its angled pylon pierces the sky to a height of 139 metres. It gets its name from the famous humanist Erasmus, who was born in Rotterdam in 1469.

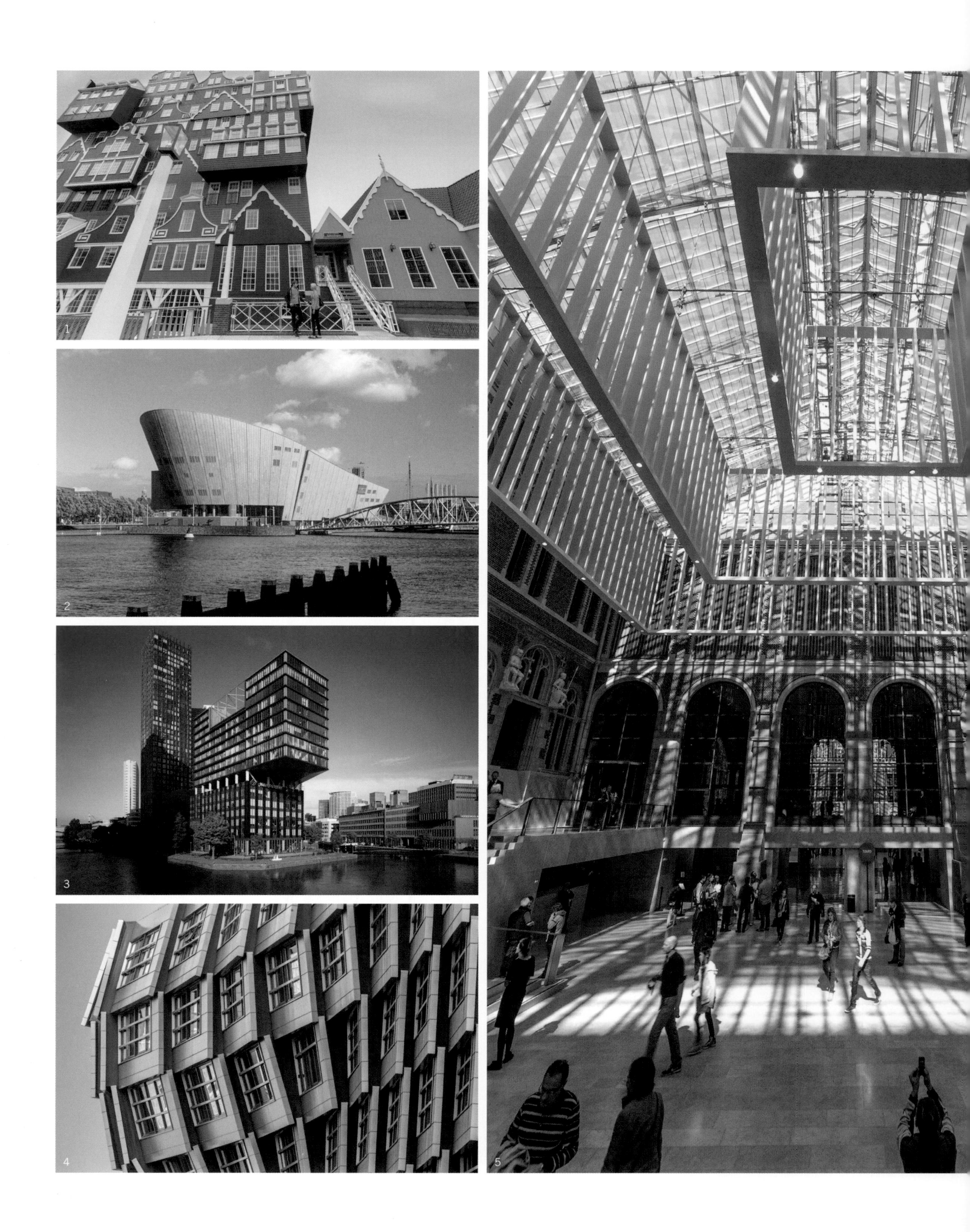
1
2
3
4
5

6

4

# People

## 'Typically Dutch!' we foreigners exclaim in exasperation. 'Typically Dutch!' say the Dutch with pride. The Dutch population totals 16.8 million, with almost as many stereotypes.

Although there is undoubtedly an element of truth in each of these stereotypes, put together they give only a vague impression of the real Dutchman. In fact, the 'typical Dutchman' probably does not exist, though we can point to a number of qualities which are characteristic of 'Homo Neerlandicus'.

**A well-ordered paradise**

A foreigner arriving in the Netherlands by plane learns one fundamental characteristic of the Dutch before he even lands. Below him, a model of order and regularity unfurls; a patchwork quilt of fields and meadows, divided by waterways, straight as arrows, and villages and housing estates laid out with geometric precision. It is immediately obvious that in designing their country, the Dutch have left nothing to chance. With their passion for organisation, they have created a neat, well-ordered paradise.

In an overcrowded country – the Netherlands is one of the most densely populated in the world – a talent for organisation is an absolute necessity and for centuries, the country's geographical location made great demands on these powers of organisation. This land, at the mercy of the whims of the sea, was like a house declared unfit to live in. Restoring and maintaining it demanded co-operation and consultation and stimulated the Dutch to carry out their dealings in an orderly and precise manner. There is no doubt that the character of the Dutch was largely determined by their country's extraordinary geographical circumstances.

**International orientation**

The Dutch owe their spirit of enterprise and their international orientation to these same circumstances. They quickly learned to regard the sea not only as an enemy, but also as a source of income and as a means of communication. The Dutch were fishermen but, in particular, they were traders. The geographical position of the Netherlands by the North Sea and at the deltas of three large rivers marked the country out for commerce and the Dutch approached their vocation with conviction. The world was their back garden and during the 17th century, the tiny Netherlands dominated global trade.

The modern-day Dutch have much in common with the successful 17th-century merchants. They are enterprising and very internationally oriented;

The Dutch in their natural habitat: on the bicycle in the city, on their way to work, the store or to meet someone.

they are punctual, fair, practical, sober, hospitable and trustworthy, qualities which are of the utmost importance in the business world. They also communicate easily, they are informal and just as accessible as their own flat country, and because of their great talent for languages they are also – quite literally – easy to approach.

These qualities make the Dutch a much-desired partner internationally. They also explain why such a tiny country as the Netherlands is so strongly represented on the international stage in economics, politics, culture and sport.

**A builder of bridges**

Their natural tolerance is another essential quality that the Dutch find useful internationally. They are accustomed to respecting other people's individuality and to seeking compromise when interests clash, rather than insisting on having their own way at all costs. The Dutch are bridge builders, not only literally but also metaphorically, and they see it as self-evident that this attitude demands a certain flexibility.

In the overcrowded Netherlands, tolerance and an ability to adapt are vital, and these qualities, too, are deeply rooted in the common struggle against the sea and in the country's commercial past. The water's threat taught the Dutch to subordinate themselves to the common interest; those who did not temper their pigheadedness were guaranteed, sooner or later, to get their feet wet – or worse. And pragmatic as they were, the 17th-century merchants quickly saw the value of tolerance. After all, trade only thrives in a climate of freedom and mutual respect, and for the merchant a customer is a customer, irrespective of the colour of his or her skin or beliefs.

**A liberal nation**

The attitude of 'live and let live' is deeply embedded in the Dutch psyche; so much so that at the end of the 19th century, Dutch society 'split', as it were, into four segments, or socio-political groupings – Catholic, Protestant, social-democrat and liberal – each with its own ideological character. These groups

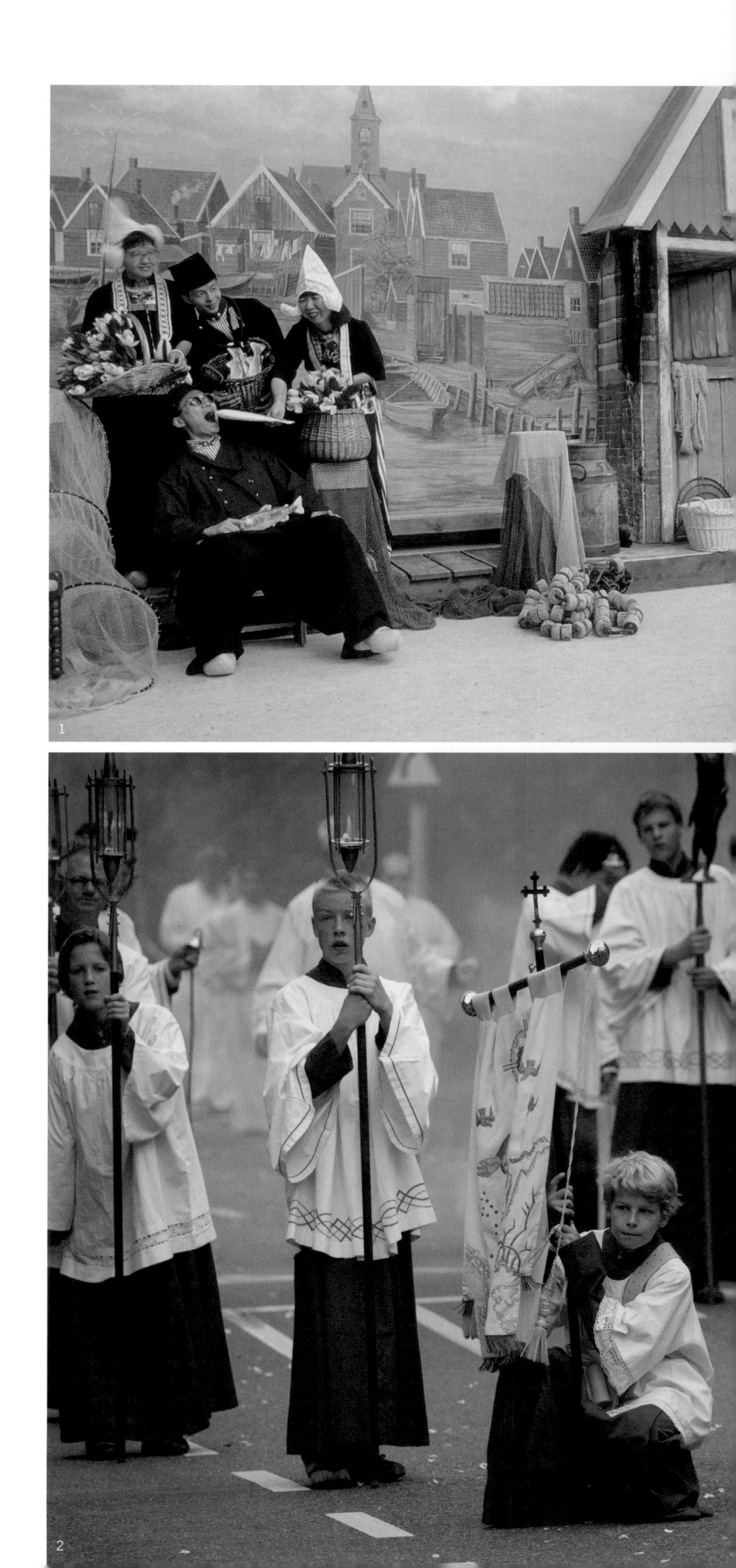

1

2

The Dutch are informal and just as accessible as their own flat country.

In Volendam, overseas tourists photograph one another in the traditional costume of the former North Holland fishing village **{1}**. The Netherlands has a rich costume tradition, in which particular attention was paid to women's lace caps and cap brooches. In the 20th century, wearing local and district costume fell out of use. In only a few places, particularly Marken and Staphorst, and to a lesser degree Urk, Spakenburg, Bunschoten, Volendam, Scheveningen, Veere **{3}** and a few other places in Zeeland, the tradition is still honoured. Elsewhere, traditional costume has now become part of the local folklore. When asked whether they would be interested in wearing a lace cap, most young Dutch women burst into laughter **{4}**.

A few of the 2,000 participants pause during the annual procession in honour of St. John the Baptist in Laren, North Holland **{2}**. The tradition of worshipping St. John the Baptist in the Catholic village dates back to the 11th century. The Netherlands was one of the most pious countries in Europe until the 1950s, but has experienced rapid secularisation since then. At present, 40% of the population still belongs to a church or mosque, although a larger section of the population, 55%, still consider themselves religious; 28% consider themselves Catholic, 18% Protestant, and 4% Islamic, while small numbers of the Dutch define themselves as Jewish, Buddhist, Hindu or Orthodox Christian.

In the overcrowded Netherlands, tolerance and an ability to adapt are vital.

had their own political parties, trade unions, schools, broadcasting organisations, societies, hospitals and newspapers and, for many of the Dutch, the world they lived in was largely limited to their own group. This unique system became much less important and eventually collapsed after 1950 under the influence of increasing secularisation, emancipation and prosperity.

A second far-reaching consequence of Dutch tolerance was that, throughout the centuries, countless immigrants found their way to the Netherlands. By around 1620, almost three quarters of the population of Amsterdam consisted of immigrants. A large part of today's Dutch population is descended from immigrants and the many 'foreign' names in the phone book – Collet, Lopes Dias, Blangé, Cohen, Hirsch Ballin, d'Ancona, Dreesmann – bear witness to this. The flames under the great melting pot of Dutch society have been rekindled since the late 1950s through the arrival of a large number of immigrants from former colonies and Mediterranean countries.

The Netherlands is still internationally recognised as a liberal and tolerant nation. Many are even of the opinion that the Netherlands is a country where anything goes. They refer to the famous Dutch tradition of tolerance, and in particular they cite the great number of coffee shops, where not much coffee is drunk but where there is a flourishing trade in other mind-expanding products. Although this view is greatly exaggerated, it is certainly true that to a large extent people can do as they please in the Netherlands.

**Good company**

However exceptional they might have been, the Dutch are unassuming about their achievements. Ostentation is alien to them. They are sober, calm and thorough, and prefer moderation and simplicity to pomp and circumstance. 'Just be ordinary, that's crazy enough,' is an old Dutch saying, and those who do not conform to this are soon regarded as being 'over the top'.

Even the Dutch Royal Family is ordinary. There is not much distance between King Willem-Alexander ('Alex', as

1 2

the people call him) and Queen Máxima and their subjects. In other kingdoms, the modest palaces of the Dutch royal family would probably be used to house the royal ceremonial coaches.

In general, the Dutch are not renowned for being born revellers and sometimes they are even imputed to be rather surly and lacking in spontaneity. They are called 'stay-at-homes' and – with reference to the Dutch climate – 'cold fish'.

The tourist who – this description in mind – arrives in the Netherlands on the King's Birthday or when an important sporting event is taking place, will wonder whether he didn't get on the wrong plane. The exuberance generated on such occasions by a merrymaking multitude of stay-at-homes and cold fish is strongly reminiscent of a Brazilian carnival.

It is true that the Dutch spend a lot of time indoors, but that is mainly forced upon them – those who do not take the weather into account are asking for trouble. But social life is no less intense because of it. There is a huge number of clubs and associations, and the many places of entertainment are generally well-filled. Moreover, the Dutch frequently visit each other; usually by appointment, true, but that is largely out of respect for each other's privacy. When the weather allows, life moves outside and in the summer months, the café patios are packed until late in the evening.

Just how companionable the Dutch are can be seen from the attention they pay to their homes and gardens. There, with great care and devotion, they create their very own, well-ordered paradises.

A woman of Turkish origin at a market in Amsterdam **{1}**. There are 3.5 million residents of foreign heritage in the Netherlands, of whom two million originate from non-Western countries. Many are from the former Dutch colonies (the Dutch East Indies, Surinam and the Dutch Antilles) or came to the Netherlands as guest workers from Mediterranean countries, particularly Morocco and Turkey.

After the declaration of independence of Indonesia (the former Dutch East Indies), 80,000 Dutch, 180,000 people of mixed Dutch-Indonesian heritage (Indos) and 12,500 Moluccans came to the Netherlands. Many of them settled in The Hague.

Around the time of the proclamation of Surinam independence in 1975, about 145,000 people, one third of the country's population, emigrated to the Netherlands. The present Surinam community consists of almost 350,000 people and is itself a mosaic of ethnic groups. The biggest of these are the Creoles (descendants of African slaves transported to Surinam by the Dutch), Hindustanis and Javanese (descendants of contract labourers from the British East Indies and Java respectively).

The Turkish (approx. 400,000) and Moroccan Dutch (370,000) are the largest ethnic groups of Mediterranean origin. Finally, 145,000 Antilleans live in the Netherlands. Of the six islands of the former Dutch Antilles, Bonaire, Saint Eustatius and Saba are municipalities of the Netherlands, while Aruba, Curaçao and Saint Maarten are autonomous countries that remain part of the Kingdom of the Netherlands.

A 'junk shop' in Utrecht **{2}**. The Dutch find it difficult to throw away 'junk'. Thriftiness from less prosperous times remains second nature to many, and items that are no longer used are taken to second hand shops or sold at flea markets.

A happy couple on the way to the popular Scheveningen beach, in South Holland, by bicycle **{3}**.

3

1
2
3
5
6
7

## Meet the Dutch

A cheerful farmer in Haastrecht, South Holland **{1}**, two girls in the snow in Utrecht **{2}**, a shopkeeper **{4}** and a woman **{5}** in The Hague, and a woman in a cheese shop in Enkhuizen, North Holland **{7}** contrast beautifully with the reflective glances of a farmer in Nuenen, North Brabant **{3}**, a woman in Delft city hall, South Holland **{6}**, and a beachcomber on the island of Texel **{8}**.

## The Dutch at work

A reed cutter in Lexmond, South Holland, is reliant on his boat to gather the harvest from his land **{1}**. Reed is grown commercially in numerous places in the Netherlands, mainly for use as thatch roofing.

Fishermen from Zierikzee in Zeeland catching lobster at Oosterschelde **{2}**. According to experts, Oosterschelde lobsters have a more subtle taste than lobsters caught elsewhere in the world.

Painter and illustrator Jeroen Dercksen poses with some of his works in his Amsterdam studio **{3}**.

Menno and Tewis Simons at their business Bocca Coffee in Dronten, Flevoland **{4}**. The brothers specialise in quality coffees and select, ship, roast, pack and sell their products themselves.

A winegrower harvesting grapes at the Apostelhoeve vineyard in Maastricht in the province of Limburg **{5}**. Dutch viticulture is undergoing rapid development and there are about 130 commercial vineyards across the country. The vast majority of those are in South Limburg, where the hills and fertile loess soil provide ideal conditions for wine farming.

Distillers Bas Lubberhuizen and Henk Raaff in their artisanal distillery in Varik, Gelderland **{6}**. The fruit for their 'eaux-de-vie' – apples, pears, plums, cherries, raspberries, blackcurrants and blackberries – comes from the orchards of the surrounding Betuwe area.

1

3

5

2
4
6

## Cycling

Almost by definition, the Netherlands is a country of bicycles. Not that the Dutch are often favourites in the Tour de France – they lose too much time in the mountains for that – but the country does have the most bicycles per head of population in the world, amounting to more than one bicycle for each inhabitant. Many Dutch own more than one – an 'ordinary' one for everyday use, and a 'best' one for cycle trips, a favourite form of relaxation which owes much of its popularity to the flatness of the Dutch countryside. People enjoying a bike ride, such as here on a dyke along the Markermeer in North Holland **{1}**, in Middenbeemster (North Holland) **{2}**, near Katwijk (North Holland) **{4}**, near Reeuwijk in South Holland **{6}** and near Echt in Limburg **{5}**, are a familiar sight. Many Dutch also use their bicycles to get to work or go shopping, like this woman in Amsterdam **{3}**.

1

2
3
4
5
6

1

## Skating

When Jack Frost reigns and the land of water becomes a land of ice, the whole of the Netherlands gets its skates on. Practically everywhere where there is a stretch of water, races and non-competitive 'tours' are organised, even on meadows that have been specially flooded. Young children are taken to the local pond where, holding the hand of their parents or hanging on to the back of a kitchen chair, they take the first faltering steps on a slippery path that perhaps will lead to a career in competitive skating. Elsewhere, in the city, on the canals of Amsterdam **{2}**, for example, people can also enjoy skating. Experienced skaters, however, prefer to seek the openness of lakes and canals and make long trips through the magical winter landscape, for example at Kinderdijk in South Holland **{1}**.

1
UP
2
AMSTEL

## Social life

The Dutch are creatures of pleasure and have a highly developed social life. Many people belong to clubs and go out to relax in their spare time. The 'brown café', a type of bar that derives its name from the cosiness and sense of security associated with wooden panelling and furniture, has always been popular. The café Hoppe in Amsterdam **{2}** dates from 1670 and is one of the oldest brown cafés in the city. But even the brownest café, like this one on Leliegracht in Amsterdam **{1}**, has a patio, because as long as the weather allows, the Dutch prefer to sit outside, or enjoy themselves with family or friends outside the city.

On warm summer days, the population heads en masse for the coast. On the beautiful beaches of famous resorts such as Scheveningen and Zandvoort, it becomes apparent just how incredibly densely populated the Netherlands is. Most other beaches, however, like this one on the island of Texel **{4}**, are much less crowded. Others prefer the open waters of the many lakes and pools, or even the Wadden Sea **{5}**, which offers a greater sense of peace and quiet. On sunny days, many families traditionally head to the wonderful Efteling in the province of North Brabant, one of the oldest theme parks in the world. Here, the most famous trash can in the country is to be found in the form of the character of 'Holle Bolle Gijs' **{3}**, who churns out the classic rhyme 'Papier hier' (paper here) – words that every Dutch child knows.

## Van Gogh was here

Vincent van Gogh (1853-1890) is perhaps the most famous of the many well-known Dutch masters. His very personal and powerful work appeals to everybody's imagination and, of course, the story of his life reads like a grand drama. The suicide of this unhappy, emotional man undoubtedly contributed to his fame, but more important is the undisputed quality of his extensive oeuvre, which was created in only ten years.

In Arles (France) during the last two years of his life, he made more than four hundred paintings. The brilliant use of colour in these later works forms a sharp contrast with his somewhat sober early work.

At the beginning of his career, he depicted, among other things, the harshness of Brabant farming life in his birthplace of Zundert, and close by in Nuenen, where his parents later resided. In these places, many of the subjects he painted and the ambience he captured so perfectly have been preserved **{2, 3}**. Van Gogh immortalised De Roosdonck windmill **{1}** in seven illustrations. In Nuenen he also created his first masterpiece, 'The Potato Eaters'. The famous painting inspired photographer Jurjen Drenth to take a picture of a Nuenen peasant family at mealtime **{4}**. Their dining room strongly resembles the room depicted by Van Gogh, and like Van Gogh's potato eaters, their living conditions are relatively harsh, and their dinner consists of potatoes, i.e. French fries.

The collections in the Van Gogh Museum in Amsterdam and the Kröller-Müller Museum in Otterlo in the province of Gelderland give a good insight into Van Gogh's work and his significance as one of the most important founders of Modern Art.

1

2

3

4

5

# Festivities

## The Dutch are said to be rather sober. This is true to a large extent, but not altogether, for on certain occasions they really let their hair down.

Overseas, the Dutch are considered to have the reputation of being serious and reserved. However, foreign visitors to the country on King's Day or Liberation Day are in for a surprise. Crowds of exuberant Dutch dressed in orange, the national colour, celebrate in cities and villages. These events provide the ideal opportunity to see the austere Dutch really letting their hair down.

Broadly speaking, there are two types of festivities in the Netherlands: festivities of a public nature, which all have their own particular brand of 'oranjegekte' (orange madness); and other festivities, such as the typically Dutch family celebration of 'Sinterklaas' (Sint-Nicolaas), that remarkable Turkish saint from Spain who speaks Dutch perfectly, are more modest and celebrated within an intimate circle.

**Domestic conviviality**

The second category is comprised of the Christian celebrations of Easter, Whitsuntide and Christmas, as well as Sinterklaas (5 December), New Year's Eve and New Year's Day. The theme of these festivities is domestic conviviality. They are usually celebrated with family or friends and an extensive festive meal is often served.

Birthdays follow much the same pattern. The person celebrating his or her birthday traditionally treats guests to drinks and snacks, perhaps a meal, and in turn receives flowers and gifts. The 50th birthday is regarded as a milestone which justifies a much more extensive celebration. Often, the person is lured by his family and friends to a restaurant or a café, where he is treated like royalty for the whole evening.

To some extent, marriages and wedding anniversaries can be compared with birthdays, except they are generally celebrated outside the home. Before a marriage, family and friends often organise a party to celebrate the last 'free' evening of the future bride and groom. Usually, they are treated by their respective friends to a 'pub crawl'. Joking and jesting, witty gifts and a great deal of drinking are the order of the day. Instances where the bridegroom was delivered to the Registry Office on his wedding day as drunk as a lord and dressed in a gorilla costume have been known – the reason why many stag nights and hen parties take place well before the wedding day.

The Dutch have a somewhat ambivalent attitude towards celebrations within the domestic circle, combining

Celebrations in a football stadium as the Dutch national team plays an international match.

### The King's Birthday

King Willem-Alexander, Queen Máxima and their three daughters wave to the public from the balcony of the Royal Palace on Dam Square in Amsterdam **{1}**. It is 30 April 2013, half an hour after Queen Beatrix has abdicated from the throne after reigning for 33 years, making her son Willem-Alexander king. His crowning coincided with the final celebration of the queen's birthday on Queen's Day and the whole country was decked out in orange. Big celebrations took place everywhere **{3}** and people sold items they no longer needed at flea markets **{4}**. It was the perfect opportunity to immortalise oneself and partner as the new king and queen **{2}**. From now on, the Dutch will celebrate Willem-Alexander's birthday annually on King's Day, on 27 April.

The House of Orange-Nassau took the throne in 1813, although ties between the 'Oranges' and the Netherlands go back much further, to the start of the 15th century. Having been a republic for centuries, the Netherlands became a constitutional monarchy, known officially as the Kingdom of the Netherlands. The role of the head of state is largely ceremonial.

as they do the pleasure of a day off with the obligation of a family visit. Many are concerned about the 'party month' of December, in particular, and every year, newspapers and magazines devote attention to the problem.

**Public 'oranjegekte'**

Family ties are noticeably less binding during the other type of celebration – the public festivities. First and foremost, these festivities are opportunities for the sober Netherlander to really let off steam. Liberation Day (5 May) and carnival belong to this category, but the celebration of the King's Birthday (27 April) beats everything.

In many places, there are big 'free' flea markets (an excuse to clear out the attic!), street performers, concerts and sometimes fairground attractions. Throngs of people, in true party mood, shuffle from one attraction to the next and orange, the colour of the Royal House, is everywhere. In the big cities, in particular, the day comes to its conclusion in lively chaos and ends with a thunderous fireworks display. Although the Dutch are not fervent monarchists, they would not miss this national celebration for the world.

The festivities on the occasion of Liberation Day (5 May) – the commemoration of the end of the German occupation during the Second World War – are somewhat similar. On the evening before Liberation Day – 'Dodenherdenking' (the Commemoration of the Dead) – the whole country comes to a standstill as the Dutch casualties of the armed conflicts that have taken place since the beginning of the Second World War are remembered.

**Two types of carnival**

Carnival, the four-day festival of ridicule, role reversal and dressing-up that precedes Lent, is largely celebrated in the predominantly Catholic southern provinces, particularly in North Brabant and Limburg. Elsewhere, many people shrug their shoulders at what they regard as 'vulgar' amusement, although there are carnival societies present all over the country.

Besides traditional carnival, there is also a 'tropical summer carnival', based on the South American model, and celebrated in Rotterdam. Originally, this was a festival celebrated by Antilleans living in the Netherlands, but it has now grown into a magnificent multicultural festival that includes theatre, poetry and concerts. The highlight is a colourful street parade: swinging to the sounds of merengue, tumba, calypso, salsa, samba and reggae, the fantastically-costumed procession weaves its way slowly through the city.

**'Elfsteden' fever**

It is not only on the King's Birthday, Liberation Day and during carnival that the Dutch give their emotions free rein – they are also seized by 'oranjegekte' during important sports events. The successes of the national football team and the club teams Feyenoord, PSV and Ajax – since the days of the legendary Johan Cruijff the most popular and

1 2

Nothing can be compared to the fever that sweeps through the Netherlands in bitter winter weather.

successful football club in the country – invariably result in spontaneous popular celebrations.

Nothing, however, can be compared to the fever that sweeps through the Netherlands in bitter winter weather. Then, the whole country talks about nothing else but the possibility of an 'Elfstedentocht', a 200-kilometre-long skating marathon through eleven towns in Friesland, starting and finishing in the Friesian capital Leeuwarden.

This marathon is only organised in very cold winters – from 1909 to 2013, the event has taken place only fifteen times, with the last one being held in 1997 – and creates an unparalleled excitement. The media are obsessed by a single question: will the 'Tocht der Tochten' (Trek of Treks) take place? On every television channel, meteorologists discuss such topics as the relationship between the thickness of the ice and wind speed, and the volunteer officials who supervise the quality of the ice along the course become national celebrities overnight.

If eventually the go-ahead is given, at least a million Dutchmen, garlanded with musical instruments, wearing orange woolly caps and waving orange flags, converge on Friesland to cheer on and support the 16,000 participants. This is not an unnecessary luxury, because many participants suffer from exhaustion and the combination of bitter cold and strong winds, which can send the perceived temperature plummeting to -20°C. The joviality along the route is unprecedented. The Elfstedentocht is a true festival of fraternisation.

**Sinterklaas**

That said, when asked what the most popular Dutch festival is, most Dutch would not say the Elfstedentocht, but

A man with icicles in his moustache and beard pauses beneath Canterlandsebrug during an unofficial Elfstedentocht on his own {1}. The bridge across the Murk is the last on the Elfsteden route under which the participants skate. It has been embellished by artists Maree Blok and Bas Lugthart with thousands of hand-made tiles with blue glazed photos of skaters who have completed the 'Trek of Treks'. Behind the skater, his own image adorns the Elfsteden monument as a proud reminder of an achievement that captivates the whole of the Netherlands.

Musicians at the 'Jazz in de Gracht' festival in The Hague, during which professional and non-professional bands perform while they sail on the canals in boats {2}.

A cheerful woman with a bouquet of orange tulips to mark King's Day at an Amsterdam street market {3}.

rather the festival of Saint Nicholas. This is celebrated on the evening of 5 December, the eve of the anniversary of the saint's death, when gifts are distributed in the family circle in the saint's name. 'Sinterklaasavond' is above all a celebration for children, who, even though most of them know better, stubbornly insist that these gifts are not from their parents, but from the genial 'Sint' himself.

There is no satisfactory answer to the question as to how this Byzantine saint has been transformed into the friend of Dutch children. Traditionally, he is said to have lived from around 270 to 343 AD in the city of Myra in present-day Turkey, where he was bishop and performer of miracles. He owes his fame as the bringer of gifts to children to some of these miracles. Children were not his only concern, however – he was also the patron saint of sailors, traders, bankers, bakers, butchers, prostitutes, thieves and prisoners.

The Sint's reputation also appealed to the people's imagination in Europe, and for a long time in the late Middle Ages, he was the most popular saint in that part of the world. In 1087, Italian merchants even abducted his bones, which since then have rested in Bari. During the Reformation, the 'Nicolaas cult' lost its significance. Nevertheless, he retained his popularity in the Calvinist Netherlands, probably because he had already become part of Dutch family life.

The reason for this lay not only in his role of children's friend, but also in his moral significance. The Sint decided whether the children had been well-behaved, and depending on this judgement he rewarded or punished them. Naughty children were threatened with a beating or being carried off 'in Sinterklaas' sack'. Punishment was to be meted out by the Sint's trusty companion Zwarte Piet (Black Peter) – the similarity of his role with the traditional role of the devil is difficult to ignore.

Because of this moral aspect, the Sinterklaas festival is also popular among adults. They use all their imagination and ingenuity in preparing beautifully wrapped and crafted 'surprises', and writing poems to attach to them. Both gifts and poems are intended to 'reward' or 'punish' the recipient's good or bad characteristics and give people an opportunity to pull each other's legs in a manner which would be unthinkable in everyday life. And then, having relieved their feelings in this way, they return to normal, everyday life, just as they do after exuberantly celebrating the King's Birthday or an important victory on the football field.

1

2

3

4

## Sinterklaas

At the beginning of December, the Netherlands falls under the spell of the festival of Sint-Nicolaas (Saint Nicholas), which reaches its climax on 'pakjesavond' (parcels evening) on 5 December. A few weeks earlier, children greet the jovial bishop upon his arrival from Spain **{1}**. No child wonders how the Sint manages to arrive at more than one place at the same time, nor do they wonder why the Byzantine bishop arrives from Spain instead of his fatherland, present-day Turkey. The Sint's association with Spain dates from the Middle Ages, when it was regarded as exotic and the cradle of all that was beautiful and pleasant. Moreover, it was teeming with Moors, the model for the Sint's faithful helper, Zwarte Piet (Black Peter). Piet personifies the devil (black with the soot of hell) and people believed the Sint had forced him to become his servant. Even today, he represents the sterner side of Sint-Nicolaas. On 5 December, children who have been well-behaved receive presents, while naughty children risk a beating from Piet or even being taken back to Spain by Piet in his sack. While traditionally the Sint travels the country on a grey horse, modern-day Pieten use bicycles **{2}**, emphasising the thoroughly Dutch nature of the Sinterklaas festival.

If they are lucky, children are allowed to 'put a shoe out' a few times during the weeks preceding 5 December. Before they go to bed, they leave a shoe next to the heater containing a carrot or some hay for the Sint's horse **{3}**. According to tradition, the Sint rides over the rooftops at night and has his helpers put gifts into the shoes through the chimneys.

In Dutch ports, churches dedicated to Saint Nicholas serve as a reminder of his classic role as the patron saint of seafarers. In Amsterdam and Kampen, he was even elevated to patron saint of the city. A memorial on Dam Square in Amsterdam bears testament to his important historical role **{4}**.

## Christmas and New Year's

During the traditional 'Kaarsjesavond' (Evening of Candles), Gouda Market is infused with a magical atmosphere when the square and surrounding buildings are illuminated by thousands of candles and the lights of a large Christmas tree {4}. About 10 days before Christmas, the mayor switches on the lights of the tree especially imported from Norway, in the presence of thousands of onlookers. Thousands of candles flicker in the stained glass windows of the 15th century gothic town hall and surrounding premises.

Similar festivities take place in various other cities and in the countryside too, where houses are illuminated like something out of a fairytale at this time of year {2}, but nowhere is the festival of light celebrated on such a grand scale as in this South Holland city. Gouda is therefore traditionally not only known for its cheese and earthenware, but for its candles, too. 'Kaarsjesavond', nowadays officially referred to as 'Gouda by candlelight', was first organised in the 1950's and is now established as part of a comprehensive cultural programme.

The Dutch usually celebrate Christmas itself with family, with a lavish meal in stylishly decorated surroundings, in which candles and Christmas tree are essential. Both Christmas and Boxing Day are official public holidays in the Netherlands and the same applies to New Year's Day. New Year's Eve, 31 December, is usually also celebrated at home with family, with a dish of 'oliebollen' {3} and a thundering fireworks display at midnight as its climax.

A unique regional tradition at this time of the year is so-called mid-winter horn blowing, an old tradition that originated in Twente and the Achterhoek region. It is reminiscent of the Yuletide festival, the old Germanic solstice that was celebrated in this region around 21 December.

The tradition is still observed to a limited degree in the east of the Netherlands. The large wind instrument is demonstrated in some places between Advent Sunday (on or around 1 December) and Epiphany (6 January), such as here at the Openluchtmuseum Ootmarsum in Twente {1}.

## Football madness

A supporter of the Dutch national football team, dressed like a warrior from the 'Orange legion', takes a photo of his heroes from the stands **{5}**. He and his consorts in the stadium **{1, 4}** personify the joyful madness which consumes many Dutch at important football matches. This 'orange ostentation' is an emotional release with a highly playful undertone. Crazy attire is the rule rather than the exception, and under the motto 'as the twig is bent, so grows the tree', children also dress up in the national colours **{2}**.

In many cities, when the Dutch national team participates in either the European or World Cup tournaments, cafés, gardens, and sometimes even entire streets are decorated. Traditionally, the highlight of orange fever manifests itself in Goirle, in the province of North Brabant, where residents of Irenestraat wrap up their houses in orange tarpaulin during these events **{3}**. For the duration, the street is given a fitting new name: Oranjestraat (Orange Street).

1

2

3

4

5

HOLLAND

## Carnival

Carnival in Maastricht. Impressive costumes are a feature of the celebration of this exuberant Catholic festival which precedes Lent. It mainly takes place in the 'Netherlands to the south of the great rivers', particularly in the provinces of Limburg and North Brabant. The great rivers form the border between the predominantly Catholic south and the largely Protestant north, where people often regard carnival as a rather vulgar celebration. Nothing of the sort, retort seasoned carnival celebrators, who are of the opinion that the northerners base their ideas on the strange doings of their own isolated carnival associations and have not got a clue about what 'real' carnival is all about. The essence of carnival is forgetting normal, serious, everyday matters – or better still, turning them on their head. Dressing up and exuberant partying are part of it, of course, but certainly not vulgarity or coarse behaviour! But the southerners could not care less if northerners understand or not – as long as at the end of February they themselves can party in towns like Maastricht, Den Bosch, Breda or Bergen op Zoom, where the festivities often go on long after the official four days are over.

THE PARTY IS HERE!!
flower power
I LOVE YOU

The 'Night Watch Guild' from Berg and Terblijt (Limburg) in action **{1}**. The guild enacts the famous Rembrandt painting 'The Night Watch', often in a frivolous manner, and brightens up all kinds of events with its performances. The 'living painting' is known nationally and internationally.

Exuberance at the fair in Hoorn, North Holland **{2}**. Fairs are held in many cities around King's Day and Liberation Day. The largest and most well-known is in Tilburg in North Brabant. This fair has been going for over 440 years, consists of about 230 attractions and attracts 1.5 million visitors from across the whole country every year.

A footman combines work with photography at the historic Binnenhof (Inner Court) in The Hague during Prince's Day **{3}**. On the third Tuesday in September, the king attracts a great deal of interest when he travels by Golden Coach from Noordeinde Palace to the Binnenhof – the seat of government and parliament (see page 66) – to deliver the Speech from the Throne, in which the government elucidates upon its plans for the coming year.

On 1 January, participants in the traditional New Year's Dive in Scheveningen dash into the freezing North Sea **{4}**. The first New Year's Dive took place in 1960. The phenomenon has since developed into a large, playful event, organised in many places. Scheveningen is the most popular location, drawing 10,000 participants.

Participants in the Canal Parade during the annual Gay Pride in Amsterdam, an event that attracts hundreds of thousands of onlookers **{5}**. The festive manifestation of the homosexual movement emphasises the liberal climate of the Netherlands in general, and that of the capital in particular. The Netherlands was the first country in the world to allow gay marriage.

4

5

6

# Economy

## The Netherlands is a world-class nexus point for trade. Supported by an ultra-modern logistics network, with the port of Rotterdam and Schiphol airport as its showpieces, it is one of the wealthiest countries in the world.

The Netherlands is traditionally a nation of transporters and traders. Because of its geographical position on the North Sea and at the mouths of three great European rivers, it forms, as it were, a natural transit port. In the 17th century, trade brought the Netherlands unprecedented prosperity. Although the economic balance has changed fundamentally since then, the status of the Netherlands as being within the 10 to 15 wealthiest countries in the world is attributable largely to its leading role in world trade.

**From fisherman to merchant**

It was fish, not trade, that first tempted the Dutch to put to sea. But once they set sail, they discovered there was a lot more to harvest than what they hauled up in their nets. They learned to regard the sea as a highway that offered lucrative opportunities in transport and trade.

In the late Middle Ages, the Dutch gradually became the cargo carrier of Europe, and later of the world. They engaged in a flourishing trade with the Baltic countries, Southern Europe, Africa, the Far East and America. An expressive illustration of the Netherlands' powerful maritime status is the fact that, of all the ships that passed the Öresund between 1560 and 1650, more than 60% flew the Dutch flag. In around 1700, more than 800 ships sailed every year for the Baltic countries from the Holland and Zeeland provinces alone.

Dutch ships carried an unprecedented variety of products. From the Baltic countries, Norway and Sweden came grain, wood, hemp, stockfish and iron; from France, Spain and Portugal salt, wine, leather and wool; from Crete muscatel and raisins; from Smyrna carpets; from Persia silk; from Surinam sugar and coffee; from the East Indies spices, silk, indigo, cloth, carpets, diamonds, rubies, pearls, ebony, and porcelain. Furthermore, fishing and whaling remained almost as important. In April of 1690 alone, more than 200 ships set sail for Greenland, where some 1,400 whales were caught.

Wind turbines on the former island of Urk in Flevoland symbolise the traditional foundations of the Dutch economy. For centuries, the Dutch depended on the wind for their livelihoods. While Dutch merchants were busy sailing the seas, the windmills back home were helping to drain the polders and to create and maintain a versatile industry.

An inland vessel on the Rhine at Lienden, Gelderland {1}. The Netherlands has almost 400 inland harbours, and over a third of national cargo transportation takes place by inland vessel. In addition, Dutch vessels play a key role in European inland navigation. The fleet of 7,000 Dutch inland vessels is the largest and most modern on the continent.

Fishermen in the harbour of West Terschelling, cleaning their nets {2}. In bygone centuries, fishing was of great importance in the Netherlands. However, the fishing industry has suffered from over-fishing in the North Sea and the imposition of international limitations on catches.

Rapidly-expanding Schiphol, to the south west of Amsterdam, is one of the best airports in the world and a showpiece of the Dutch economy {3}. Over a hundred airlines carry 51 million passengers and 1.5 million tons of cargo from Schiphol to approximately 320 direct destinations annually, making this airport one of the largest in Europe. Schiphol is the home base of the national KLM airline, the world's oldest airline, which merged with Air France in 2003.

In the 17th century, the Netherlands possessed the first modern economy in the world.

**The Golden Age**

Trade brought unprecedented prosperity. From 1600 to 1670, the Netherlands was the richest country in Northern Europe, possessed the first modern economy in the world and was admired for its wealth and progressive, tolerant civic urban culture. Amsterdam developed into the economic, political and cultural centre of the world and along its canals rose the stately merchants' houses which still determine the monumental nature of the inner city. It is to this period that the Netherlands owes its reputation as a great maritime power, a reputation which in the 19th and 20th centuries was given a new impulse by the powerful hydraulic engineering projects carried out in the Low Countries.

This reputation partly rested on the activities – not always benign – of two renowned trading companies: the Dutch East India Company (VOC), founded in 1602 as a merger between companies in Amsterdam, Enkhuizen, Hoorn, Rotterdam, Delft and Middelburg; and the West India Company (WIC), founded in 1621. The VOC operated largely in Asia, the WIC in America and, largely in the context of the flourishing slave trade, West Africa.

The VOC in particular was successful for a long period – for more than a century and a half this multinational was the greatest enterprise in the world. One of the WIC's outstanding exploits was the setting up of the trading post of Nieuw-Amsterdam (New Amsterdam), present-day New York.

Besides being a trading nation, the Netherlands in those days was a formidable sea power, which was not averse to taking violent action when freedom of trade was threatened – three trade wars were fought with protectionist Britain. Just like the military exploits of famous admirals such as De Ruyter and Tromp, the colonial adventures of the Netherlands were also in the context of trade. It was not imperialistic but commercial motives that were at the root of the lengthy domination of the Dutch East Indies (today's Indonesia), Surinam and the Dutch Antilles.

But the Golden Age was not exclusively an age of traders and maritime heroes. Prosperity was the basis of an impressive cultural flowering. Painting, in particular, flourished, as can be seen from the collections of the Amsterdam Rijksmuseum, amongst others. Among the hundreds of Dutch masters are world

2

3

The headquarters of Unilever Netherlands in Rotterdam, called De Brug (The Bridge). Anglo-Dutch multinational Unilever is one of the world's largest suppliers of food and home and personal care products.

1
2

famous painters such as Rembrandt van Rijn, Frans Hals, Johannes Vermeer and Jan Steen, who found life much tougher when they were alive than their posthumous fame might suggest. Vermeer's work even hung on his baker's wall as security for a debt of 617 guilders.

**Late industrialization**

Economic growth stagnated in the 18th century, one reason being that more countries were transporting their own goods. For the Dutch, who largely traded in foreign goods and who did not have any meaningful domestic industries of their own, this was a heavy blow. What domestic industry there was, was concentrated in the ports and mainly involved processing imported products which were then transhipped to other countries. This imbalance meant that at the beginning of the 19th century, the Netherlands was outstripped by her arch-rival England, the cradle of the Industrial Revolution.

Countries such as Germany and Belgium were also industrialized before the Netherlands, where this process only began at the end of the 19th century. Partly because of the deep economic crisis of the 1930s, it would take until after the Second World War before the Netherlands once again ranked as one of the world's richest countries.

Then, the country experienced huge economic growth, following in the footsteps of Germany. This is shown, among other things, by the expansion of wholly or partly owned Dutch multinationals such as Philips, Unilever, Shell and Heineken, companies which brought world-wide recognition to the Netherlands.

Another important consequence of the German renaissance was that, as a port, Amsterdam was eclipsed by Rotterdam. Strategically situated, Rotterdam is the fifth largest port in the world and has an important transhipment function for the European Union. Amsterdam, the fifth largest port in Europe, is also a significant international player, as are other Dutch ports to a lesser degree.

Multinationals such as Philips, Unilever, Shell and Heineken, brought world-wide recognition to the Netherlands.

Dutch industry is specialised in the production of high-quality products, but because of the scarcity of raw materials – other than natural gas, which makes an important contribution to the national treasury – it is highly dependent on other countries. For this reason, a number of important industries, particularly the petrochemical and iron and steel industries, are situated on, or near, the coast. Another feature is that, because of the limited domestic market, the large industrial concerns are very internationally oriented. The Netherlands is the headquarters of a strikingly large number of multinational enterprises, proving once again that industry is closely linked to distribution and transport.

### The Flying Dutchman

The face of the Dutch economy abroad is not only determined by companies such as Philips, but also by agricultural products, ranging from bulbs to pedigree Friesian cattle. The Netherlands is one of the top three exporters of agricultural products in the world. Vegetables, cheese and beer are products that the Netherlands exports more of than any other country. This is partly due to the high productivity of Dutch agriculture, which is ultramodern, large-scale, capital-intensive and labour-extensive. Today, less than 3% of the Dutch earn their living in the agricultural sector, as opposed to more than 50% in 1900.

Horticultural productivity is also high. Hothouse cultivation has increased enormously, and for many foreigners the imposing 'glass city' in the Westland is just as familiar an image as the airport of Schiphol or the port of Rotterdam, the transit points which are so important for the export of Dutch specialities.

The strong growth of these 'mainports' illustrates that the trade, transport, distribution and service industries remain of inestimable importance to the Dutch economy. Schiphol, for years one of the world's best airports, plays an important role in both passenger and cargo transport and is the home base of the world's oldest airline, 'Flying Dutchman' KLM.

Just as in the 17th century, the tiny Netherlands is a trade centre with great allure, particularly as far as high-quality products are concerned. It is significant that the Netherlands houses more international distribution centres than any other European country and it is no wonder that the accessibility of foreign markets and the lifting of trade barriers are still themes which concern the Dutch more than most people. It is for this reason the Netherlands has always been a firm supporter of European integration. Although the days when the Netherlands drummed up her admirals to enforce freedom of trade are gone for good, sometimes the Dutch are not all that far removed from their 17th-century merchant ancestors.

An engine driver for the Nederlandse Spoorwegen (NS), the most important railway operator in the country {1}. The micro-meshed Dutch railway grid is the busiest track in the European Union, and the busiest in the world apart from Switzerland and Japan.

Electricians making repairs to the top of a power pylon in Zwolle, Overijssel {2}.

Drilling platforms in the North Sea near Texel island {3}.

A vision from the 17th century: Zaanse Schans near Zaandijk in North Holland. With its seven windmills and traditional homes and warehouses, this little village is a reminder of the hey-day of the Zaanstreek, the oldest industrial region in the world. The first saw-mill was built in 1596 and was the start of what became an extensive and varied industrial area. A few decades later, there were about 600 mills in the region and by the 18th century there were more than 1,000. They sawed Norwegian and German timber, mixed paint pigments, polished marble, processed hemp, pressed oil, stamped tobacco, treated paper and lead, and ground foodstuffs such as cocoa, mustard and grain.

The Zaanstreek was a rich industrial region. Its shipyards were world-renowned; in 1797, the Russian Tsar Peter the Great came to Zaandam to study ship-building. In the middle of the 19th century, however, the mills made way for factories, which worked on steam power. This phase in Zaanse history will forever be linked with the founding of famous Dutch provisions companies such as Verkade, Honig, Duyvis and Albert Heijn.

The mills and buildings in the Zaanse Schans are a reminder of the days when people here literally lived off the wind. They are all authentic and mostly taken from other places in the Zaanstreek and rebuilt here on the Schans. Although many are accessible to the general public, they are not museums. People live and – according to established Zaanse custom – work here.

## Flower Power

Nowhere is the saying 'your money's worth more at the market' more applicable than at the Dutch flower markets, of which the one in Amsterdam is the best known, but Utrecht's the loveliest **{1}**. In a country where the cultivation of bulbs and flowers has been raised to an art form, flowers are cheaper and more generally available than anywhere else in the world.

Bulbs have been studied **{5}** and cultivated in the Netherlands since the end of the 16th century. At that time, the tulip was the favourite. From 1636 to 1637, the lively bulb trade led to extravagant speculation and many a citizen lost all he possessed.

The Netherlands is the largest producer of cut flowers and plants and accounts for over half of all global trade. The centre of today's trade in cut flowers and pot plants is the FloraHolland flower auction, which consists of five sites and is the biggest flower auction in the world **{4, 6}**. At least 12.5 billion flowers and pot plants change hands here every year – roses being by far the favourite. The bulk of the flowers sold goes abroad, the remainder is sold to Dutch consumers via florists such as this one in Amsterdam **{3}**.

Ornamental plant cultivation largely takes place in greenhouses, like this one in Moerkapelle, South Holland **{2}**, in contrast to bulb cultivation, which covers an area of about 25,000 hectares. The most cultivated bulbs are the tulip, lily, narcissus, gladiola and hyacinth and these, too, are exported to the four corners of the world. The Netherlands accounts for 75% of the global bulb trade and annually about 6.5 billion bulbs are exported.

2

3

4

5

T3
6

et vis van Toe
goed
KAAS

1

2

3

4

5

## Say cheese

Bustling trade at the cheese market of the city of Gouda **{1}** – a name that is music to the ears of cheese lovers worldwide. The Netherlands is the most important cheese market in the world. Of the 800 million kilograms produced there annually, about 80% is exported, making the Netherlands by far the largest cheese exporter in the world. In addition, the Dutch themselves consume more than 15 kilograms of it per person on an annual basis.

Archaeological finds show that the Dutch were already making cheese thousands of years ago. Furthermore, in the 1th century BC, Julius Caesar himself described the habit of consuming cheese that had been observed in the Low Countries. At that time, famous cheese producing centres like Gouda and Edam did not yet exist. Responsible for 60% of the national production, Gouda cheese is the most commonly produced variety, while the distinctive round cheeses from Edam are more famous. These are made in a bowl-shaped mould called a 'kaaskop' (cheese head), a word used in Belgium and other countries as a disparaging name for the Dutch.

The cheese industry is state-of-the-art and exists on a massive scale. However, there are still plenty of smaller, traditional cheese producers around, such as these cheese farms in Vlist **{2}** and Haastrecht **{5}**, both in the province of South Holland, and this one near Leusden in the province of Utrecht **{3}**. Today, the atmospheric cheese markets in Gouda in South Holland, and in Edam **{4}** and Alkmaar in North Holland are famous tourist attraction. In Alkmaar and Gouda, as well as in several other towns, cheese museums are on hand to teach overseas visitors everything they could want to know about cheese production.

## Agriculture

Although a large part of the Netherlands is utilized for agriculture, such as for the sprawling Apostelhoeve vineyard in South Limburg **{1}**, very few Dutch (less than 3%) actually earn their living from the land. The farming industry is large-scale and ultramodern. For many activities, such as harvesting sugar-beet near Vijfhuizen, North Holland **{3}**, there are hardly any human beings needed nowadays.

Modernisation of agriculture has led to a great increase in production and there are few countries where the yield per hectare is greater than in the Netherlands. Hothouse cultivation in the Westland **{2}** is a good example of modern management. Vegetables, fruit and plants, mainly for export, are grown in the 'glass city' around Naaldwijk in South Holland.

The cattle breeding sector is just as modern. Breeders strive to continuously improve the quality of the cattle using the most modern breeding methods. Cattle breeding is an extremely serious industry and, furthermore, big business. Dutch cattle **{4}** are world champions in the production of milk and symbolise the world-famous dairy industry. The sperm of breeding bulls also generates a good income. There are over 4 million cattle in the Netherlands, including over 1.5 million dairy cows.

1
2
4

3.

## The Golden Age

The 17th century – or to be more exact the period between about 1585 and 1670 – has gone down in history as the 'Golden Age'. It was a time in which the Netherlands experienced enormous economic expansion and Amsterdam grew into a global trading centre. It was during this period that many of the characteristic canal houses in the capital **{6}** were built by immensely wealthy merchants. At the same time, the enduringly impressive building De Waag – originally a 15th-century city gate – was repurposed as the city's premier weighing-house **{1}**.

Although the prosperity was partly due to the flourishing fishing industry, processing industries and agriculture, it was the achievements of the merchant trading fleet, in particular those of the Dutch East India Company (VOC), which most appeal to the imagination. This enterprise, founded in 1602, was the world's first multinational company and for more than one and a half centuries it dominated trade in East Asia. Chinese porcelain imported by the VOC was the source of inspiration for the Delft pottery industry, which applied itself to Asian imitations as well as to typical Dutch products **{2}**. Delft Blue was known throughout Europe and is still manufactured according to traditional methods.

The ships of the VOC – to our eyes hardly more than cockleshells – decorate many a façade, including this 17th-century building in Medemblik, North Holland **{4}**. A replica of the VOC ship 'De Amsterdam' can be seen in front of the Maritime Museum in Amsterdam **{5, 7}**.

The gold of the Golden Age formed the basis for a great cultural flourishing, which expressed itself in painting, in particular. Perhaps the true symbol of this is Rembrandt's masterpiece 'De Nachtwacht', a 'schuttersstuk' (a painting of civilian militia), dating from 1642 **{3}**. It is one of the high points of the collection of the Amsterdam Rijksmuseum.

1

2

3

7

## A proud port

The port of Rotterdam is by far the largest in Europe and the fifth largest in the world. Approximately 450 million tons of goods are handled here every year **{1, 3, 4, 5}**. About 80% of this is intended for transhipment, most of it abroad. The port owes its important 'hub' function to its excellent links to the North Sea and the European hinterland, as well as to its good road and rail connections and its proximity to Rotterdam The Hague Airport and Schiphol. Crude oil accounts for about a quarter of shipments. This is discharged in eight petroleum docks and processed in huge refineries within the harbour area. Furthermore, as Rotterdam is also an important industrial centre, the petrochemical industries are situated in the immediate vicinity **{6}**.

The completion of the 18-kilometre long Nieuwe Waterweg in 1872 was a great step in Rotterdam's development into a port of global importance. At the same time, in central Rotterdam **{2}**, a start was made on the development of the south bank of the Maas. One building here was the proud head office of the Holland-America Line, now the Hotel New York. Later, the port also grew in a westerly direction. In 1931, the Waalhaven was completed, at that time the biggest dock in the world.

Further expansion followed immediately after the Second World War with the Botlek, Europoort – a name which indicated that Rotterdam now regarded itself as being the 'Poort naar Europa' (Gateway to Europe) – and the Maasvlakte, where an ultramodern container port was built. In 2012, construction of Maasvlakte 2 was completed, further extending the harbour into the North Sea. The harbour is now 42 kilometres in length and measures around 12,500 hectares.

1

2

4
CONTAINERSHIPS VIII
UBC
5
HAMBURG SÜD
6

**Martijn de Rooi** is a writer, journalist and copywriter and publishes books, reports, columns and book reviews {1}. After graduating with distinction as a sociologist from Utrecht University, he was associated with this university as a researcher. As a journalist, editor and editor-in-chief he worked for various magazines, publishers and broadcasting networks in the Netherlands and abroad. As a copywriter, he regularly works for leading companies and government departments.
De Rooi wrote a number of books on Holland. Among them *The Dutch, I presume?*, *The Rembrandt Guide*, *Visions of the Netherlands*, *How to survive Holland* and the children's book *Hans Brinker*. His books on international destinations include *Sahara – Land beyond Imagination* and travel guides on Egypt, Indonesia and Cyprus. Among the corporate publications De Rooi wrote is the book *Unilever Matters*.

**Jurjen Drenth** is well-known for the natural, atmospheric style of his photography {2}. He broke through thanks to his attractive coverage of the Netherlands, which he photographed in all its versatility. His unique series on the famous Dutch painters Rembrandt, Vermeer and Van Gogh drew world-wide attention.
Reports from Drenth on the Netherlands and many other countries were published in leading international journals, such as *National Geographic* and *Traveler*. He also supplied the photography for the books *Exploring the Netherlands*, *The Dutch, I Presume?*, *Dutch Delight* and *The Rembrandt Guide*. Furthermore, Drenth regularly works for government departments, the Netherlands Board of Tourism and Conventions, The Hague and Utrecht City Marketing, and leading companies such as Unilever, KLM (Royal Dutch Airlines), NS (Dutch Railways) and KPN (Royal Mail and Telecom).